action for racial equality in the early years

understanding the past, thinking about the present, planning for the future

••••••••••••••••••••••••••

a practical handbook for early years workers

Jane Lane

the national
early years
network

In memory of Kathleen Wsama, who talked about her life of challenging racism in the East End of London between the wars in a BBC *Opinions* programme during the early 1980s, moving many of us to tears. And for my father, who always stood up against injustice and encouraged me to think critically about it from an early age. He is my mentor.

'How society rids itself of such attitudes is not something which we can prescribe, except to stress the need for education and example at the youngest age, and an overall attitude of "zero tolerance" of racism within our society.'

Report of the Stephen Lawrence Inquiry (1999) para. 7.42

About the author

Jane Lane is the co-ordinator of the Early Years Trainers Anti Racist Network (EYTARN). She was formerly an education officer at the Commission for Racial Equality and was largely responsible for writing their 1996 publication *From cradle to school: a practical guide to racial equality in early childhood education and care.*

Acknowledgements

The author wishes to thank those people who gave their time to read this book during preparation, all of whom made constructive and helpful comments. They are Margaret Andrews, Rashida Baig, Babette Brown, Cressida Evans, Sue Griffin, Pat Joseph, Cath Sinclair and Norma Wildman. Others who gave their time to discuss particular issues are Mary Jane Drummond, Lucy Davies, Rose Drury, Alison Hatt, Tina Hyder, Gerri Ross and Greta Sandler.

Action for racial equality in the early years was funded by the National Lottery Charities Board.

ISBN: 1 870985 45 1

© National Early Years Network 1999

All rights reserved. This publication is copyright, but may be reproduced by any method without fee or prior permission for use with staff, children or students, but not for resale. For copying in any other circumstances prior written permission must be obtained from the publisher and a fee may be payable.

Designed and printed by Expression, IP23 8HH

Contents

Introduction *4*
The purpose of this handbook *4*
Terms used in this handbook *4*

1 What do we mean by prejudice and discrimination? *6*
Prejudice and discrimination *6*
Prejudice into practice *8*
Prejudice, discrimination and young children *9*
Prejudice, discrimination and adults *11*
The process of change *11*

2 How children learn about racism *12*
Learning to be prejudiced *12*
Living in mainly 'white' areas *14*

3 Talking about racism *16*
Meanings can change *16*
Words used for talking about racism *16*
What these terms really mean *18*
Talking the same language *19*

4 Learning from the past *20*
Books and research on child development *21*
The role of the media *22*
Language *22*
Multiculturalism *25*
Lessons learned in the early years field *25*

5 Thinking about racial equality *27*
Child-rearing practices *27*
Identity and self-esteem *28*
Knowing about history and culture *29*
The problems in talking about racism *30*

6 Developing a policy for racial equality *33*
Developing a policy without support *34*
Early years settings and families *34*
Creating a no-blame culture *38*
Establishing a multiracial workforce *40*
Working with young children *41*
Religion *44*

7 The law on racial equality *46*
Guidance, consultation documents and reviews *46*
Major legislation *47*
    Race Relations Act 1976 *47*
    The Children Act 1989 *50*

8 Challenging racism and harassment *52*
Immediate responses to racist incidents *52*
Having a policy on harassment *54*

9 Planning for equality across the early years service *56*
A framework of interlinked components *57*
Making it all work *65*

Useful addresses and contacts *66*

Notes *68*

Introduction

An equal society offers equal chances and equal treatment to all its members. It works towards removing any barriers that discriminate against people or hold back equality.

To feel secure, confident, comfortable, content and able to pursue our ambitions as members of society, we need to be valued for ourselves, to be respected and treated with dignity and fairness. For example, in Britain we generally like to be served in a shop in the order in which we arrived. If there are many of us we form a queue, and people barging to the front are likely to be met with some hostility. Most of us think that we should have equal access to health treatment, whatever our financial situation. We want teachers and carers to give each of our children an equal chance to succeed at school and in early years settings. And we expect to be paid a reasonable wage for our work and cared for if we are ill.

But do we expect everyone else to be treated in the same way as we expect to be treated? Is everyone else treated fairly? And are we treated fairly ourselves?

Looking around, we can see that some people do not have the same chances as others – they are not treated as they would like to be. In fact, *we* may not be treated as we would like to be. In considering ourselves, how much are we prepared and able to get equal chances for ourselves? How far are we prepared to consider others who may have fewer chances than we have?

Whatever our individual wishes, they are likely to be influenced by the beliefs, values and attitudes of our society. Thinking about equality usually means examining the world around us, rethinking what we do, what we say and how the influences on our lives have determined our attitudes and behaviour.

The purpose of this handbook

It is well known that the early years of a child's life are critical for learning the basic skills that enable them to benefit from education in school and in life generally. Anything which interferes with this learning process, or which distorts reality, may have long-term consequences.

Adults are in a position to exert a strong influence on children's learning, including their attitudes to differences. If prejudice and discrimination are to be fully addressed, it is important to develop strategies to counter prejudicial attitudes and behaviour among adults as well as children. Children have a right not to learn such negative attitudes and not to be subjected to any behaviour resulting from them.

Being prejudiced denies children access to many of life's experiences and opportunities, but learning *not* to be prejudiced opens up possibilities for the child – and has benefits for everyone else too.

All children learn to categorise things. They learn to make judgements. Evidence shows that children as young as two years old are able to use racial cues as a basis for identification and categorisation. They are learning whose physical appearance is most valued by society and, as they grow up, some may discriminate against the people who are seen as less valuable.

Learning to respect the opinions, differences and needs of others is an important aspect of children's overall social development, and valuing racial differences is just one aspect of this. Whatever their racial attitudes, children are capable of considering another point of view. They can build up a balanced interpretation of what they have already learned when provided with correct information in a non-threatening atmosphere where everyone has equal value. In this kind of environment, children can learn to consider different opinions, analyse them and make up their own minds.

Action for racial equality in the early years looks at general issues of fairness and equality, and how they should be an integral part of early years services. It discusses specific issues of racial prejudice and the behaviour that may result from them, and focuses on the practices that may hinder equality in early years services and settings in Britain. These practices constitute racism.

Terms used in this handbook

For a detailed look at the words used when talking about racial equality and racism, see pages 16–19.

The meaning of 'black' and 'white'

The term **black** is used here in a political sense, to include all people who are likely to be discriminated against because of their skin colour. It includes African, African-Caribbean and South Asian people, and those people from other minority ethnic communities where skin colour is a determining factor. Using the term 'black' is not an ideal alternative to listing every minority ethnic group throughout the book, but it removes the need for clumsy repetition. When a specific group of people is being referred to, this is made clear.

To a certain extent, the term 'black' is being used here for simplicity. It should *never* be imposed on a child, as some families may feel that this confuses a child's sense of identity. For example, some families from South Asia do not wish to be called black, and this should be respected.

The term **white** is also used here in its political sense. It includes all those people who are not usually discriminated against because of their skin colour. Travellers, Irish and Jewish people who are white are exceptions to this as they often experience discrimination. The word 'white' covers those people of European origin and those who migrated from Europe to places like New Zealand, Australia, Canada, some South American countries, South Africa and the United States of America. Of course, there are also black people living in these countries.

Describing the early years environment

In the early years field, children are cared for and educated in a variety of settings, including nurseries, day nurseries, nursery schools, nursery classes, crèches, playgroups, pre-schools, kindergartens, family centres, drop-in centres parent and toddler clubs, after-school clubs and with childminders. In this text, the phrase **early years setting** is used to cover all the above, except where otherwise stated. Young children are also cared for in their homes, but an early years setting does not seem an appropriate term to use for this because a child's home is much more than a formal setting for care and education.

The phrase **people who work with children** is used to refer to the wide variety of people working in the early years field. It includes childminders, practitioners, carers, teachers, educators, researchers, nursery nurses, support staff, visiting staff, supervisors, caterers, cleaners, officers, helpers, managers, clerical staff and receptionists.

Introduction | **5**

1 | What do we mean by prejudice and discrimination?

There are many forms of inequality in our society. They include unequal treatment on the grounds of being a woman, a black person, from a minority ethnic group, from a particular social group or class, being a Gypsy, a Jewish person, an Irish person, a Traveller, being disabled, homosexual, poor, homeless, a refugee or asylum-seeker, living in a particular place, having a particular accent or dialect, dressing in a particular way or attending a particular kind of school.

There are laws in Britain that make discrimination on grounds of sex, 'race' or disability unlawful. Early Years Development and Childcare Plans are expected to cover the equal opportunity strategy and ensure equality of access and opportunity, according to the planning guidance from the Department for Education and Employment.[1]

For many people, who consider themselves sympathetic or thoughtful, issues of equal opportunity don't seem to have any relevance to the way young children are brought up or cared for at this early stage. People who work with children do the best for all the children in their care. Most people would like the world to be a place where issues of equality were irrelevant, a place where everyone already has an equal place in society. If that was the case, there would be no need to even consider these matters.

But in the real world everyone is not equal. Many people, for all sorts of reasons, have to struggle for the necessities of life that others take for granted. They do not have the same life chances as others. For instance, many deaf people get left out of events because it is assumed that they cannot take part, and wheelchair users are generally prevented from using public transport because buses and trains are not fitted with platforms that would allow them access.

Our concern here is with young children. They are the most vulnerable members of our society, and everyone working with them needs to strive for them all to be given an equal chance to succeed and fulfil their dreams. But equality of opportunity does not yet exist and it is therefore important that all of us involved with young children consider how to achieve it.

Prejudice and discrimination

Prejudice – literally – is forming an opinion about a person with little or no information or evidence on which to base that opinion. It means that person is pre-judged by others, maybe even before they have met.

Anyone can be prejudiced. Men and women can be prejudiced. Black and white people can be prejudiced. Disabled and able-bodied people can be prejudiced. Lesbian and gay people can be prejudiced. People from all social classes can be prejudiced. Rich and poor, homeless and housed, employed and unemployed, old and young, British and 'foreign', religious and non-religious; all people can be prejudiced against any other group of people, not because of who they are but simply because they are perceived to be a member of a certain group.

Many people experience prejudice against themselves and anyone can be prejudiced. But this does not make it any better and does not make it right. The reality is that some people are more prejudiced than others and some people experience more prejudice than others.

Why should any of us be prejudiced against others?

- Is it because we do not understand them?
- Is it because we think they are less deserving and getting the benefit of something that they shouldn't?
- Is it because we think they have not 'earned' privileges we think they might have?
- Is it because we are afraid of something – of losing our own identity, culture or way of life?
- Do we really think we are superior to some others?
- Do we know that we are prejudiced?
- Do we mind if someone says that we are prejudiced?

The reasons for people being prejudiced are complex and varied, but they include our different histories and the legacies they leave, different economic and social situations, different power relationships between people and groups, and ignorance and misinformation. As a result of all these factors, inequality has become embedded in the fabric of our

6 | Action for racial equality in the early years

society and 'accepted' as part of the way that it is organised. Inequality is part of the system.

Prejudice and discrimination exist because they are allowed to exist. Prejudiced attitudes and behaviour, reinforcing and perpetuating inequalities, are passed from generation to generation in subtle ways and are largely unrecognised. It is only when attitudes are expressed in behaviour that discrimination occurs.

Whatever the reasons, if any action resulting from prejudice disadvantages or discriminates against another person, that action is morally wrong. If it is covered by legislation, it may also be unlawful. Even when no obvious prejudice is involved, it is wrong and may still be unlawful.

Forms of discrimination

Some aspects of inequality are obvious, such as overtly prejudiced comments and discriminatory behaviour. For example, some people believe that women cannot make good Members of Parliament, and they believe this because they are prejudiced against women doing that sort of work.

Other forms of inequality are not so obvious. They are hidden in complex practices and procedures or built into the way society has been organised over long periods of time. For example, conference venues with no toilet access for disabled people make it impossible for people in wheelchairs to attend conferences that are held there. No single person deliberately arranged for this to happen, but the effect is that some disabled people are being discriminated against, if unintentionally. This is sometimes called **institutional discrimination** (see page 8).

Women are more often responsible for running a home and looking after children than men. The provision of affordable childcare is still insufficient so that, overall, women with children have fewer opportunities and greater difficulties in running a career. They are discriminated against because of the traditional structures in our society. This is sometimes called **structural discrimination** (see pages 8–9).

Stereotypes

Prejudice is sometimes associated with stereotyping. Most people make assumptions about others from their outward appearances. On seeing someone for the first time, most people move into an almost unconscious mode of assessing what they are like, what they do and what are their specific 'identifying' characteristics. For example,

people who see a white man, with tattoos, pierced ears and a shaved head might assume that he is a skinhead, but he may have no association whatever with racist people or racist views. Many young black men say that they notice white women clutching their handbags more tightly in their presence. The stereotype is that black men are muggers and the consequence is to make them feel as if they are a threat to 'civilised' society. Such feelings do not contribute to a society based on equal respect.

Our assumptions may mean that we treat people unfairly. For example, if we assume that Asian fathers always speak and act on behalf of their families, we may not even bother to find out what Asian mothers think. This may lead to Asian boys being treated differently from girls.

Joe, a four-year-old African-Caribbean boy, joins a local playgroup. There is only one other black child, a girl, and he doesn't know any of the other children. He feels a bit shy and so plays alone on a bicycle for a few minutes. No one interrupts him and he moves on to play on the slide. He then returns to the bicycle. He gets braver and starts going quite fast, riding it all over the place.

One of the playgroup workers, Rita, has a particular responsibility for Joe and is pleased to see him occupying himself. Although she would not actually say it, she has some idea that black boys have difficulty in concentrating and that they like physical activity.

Several days later, Joe is still mainly occupied on the wheeled toys. No one suggests that he plays elsewhere, with jigsaws or painting or looking at books. No other child is unsupervised in this way. Because Rita's assumption, based on a stereotype, is that Joe is doing what he is best at doing and what he likes doing, she is happy for him and happy that he appears to be content. But Joe has had no opportunity to develop learning skills or to co-operate with other children. Rita's assumptions have helped to create the behaviour that Joe is displaying – and he is being denied access to vital parts of his all-round development.

Rita's discrimination is unintentional, but it is based on hidden stereotyped attitudes that can remain hidden and may have serious and long-term consequences.

Stereotyping is about believing that the characteristics of one person are found in all

What do we mean by prejudice and discrimination? | **7**

members of the group to which that person belongs, based on some notion that may or may not have an element of truth in it. Stereotyping may be about 'good', 'neutral' or 'bad' characteristics. The point is that all stereotypes are untrue:

- Asian girls are *not all* passive;
- African-Caribbean boys are *not all* good at sport;
- *not all* blind people love dogs;
- working class parents are *not all* indifferent to education;
- *not all* Irish men drink a lot and neither do they *all* have the gift of the gab;
- *not all* Jewish people are rich; and
- girls are *not all* incapable of playing football.

Prejudice can 'allow' groups of children to be stereotyped. For example, whole cultural groups of children may be labelled as being 'not properly brought up'. Their families may be criticised for 'not taking them to the park', 'not teaching them to eat properly', 'forcing their religion on their children' or 'bringing them up differently'.

Prejudice into practice

Some actions can be seen to be the direct result of prejudice. For example, if the governing body of a nursery school refuses to consider a man's application for a job simply because he is a man – because they think that women work better than men with young children – that is discrimination due to sex-based prejudice. It is sex discrimination and would be unlawful.

Other discriminatory actions may not result directly from individual prejudicial attitudes. They may be so embedded in the system that few people really think about them. Even so, they have a clear effect on particular groups of people. These forms of discrimination are institutional and structural. They are part of society and not the result of an individual's deliberate action.

Institutional discrimination

This is not usually a result of deliberate, individual action. It occurs when long-established practices and procedures, which may be official or unofficial, combine with thoughtless, (often unconscious) prejudice, stereotyping and cultural assumptions to produce discrimination. While many members of the institution may believe they are not personally prejudiced or that they do not hold stereotyped attitudes, their failure to recognise or challenge forms of discrimination within the institution means that they are part of the institutional discrimination. Only those people

who recognise and challenge racism can genuinely claim to be exceptions.

Institutional discrimination in the early years

An early years setting that operates a waiting list and offers places on a first-come-first-served basis, with those at the top of the list having priority, may well be operating institutional discrimination.

At first sight the waiting list seems as fair a method as any, but in practice families who are unfamiliar with the concept of waiting lists do not put their children's names down as early as others. This means that their children will be lower on the list and be less likely to gain a place than children from families who are familiar with the system. People who are unfamiliar with the system are likely to include families:

- where English is not the first language;
- that have recently arrived in Britain (and do not yet know about early years organisations); or
- who move about a lot.

This will disproportionately affect Travellers, refugees and asylum seekers, and Asian and other minority ethnic families. There may be no specific intention to give them less of a chance but that will be the effect. This does not mean that waiting lists should be dispensed with altogether, as they are useful sources of information about the people who wish to use the setting. However, fairer ways of organising admissions should be implemented alongside waiting lists, and attempts made to contact members of all groups living in the community.

Structural discrimination

This occurs as a result of the way society is structured and the way power is positioned. For example, in the 1950s and 1960s the industrialised areas of Britain specifically recruited South Asian and African-Caribbean workers because industrial production increased rapidly to help recovery after the Second World War. These were the very areas that experienced severe decline in manufacturing in the 1980s. Despite 20 or 30 years in the regions, the 'immigrant' population was still not established in the community in terms of such things as secure housing, and so they suffered disproportionately from the effects of long-term unemployment during the 1980s.

Structural discrimination in the early years

A disproportionate number of African-Caribbean mothers have to work long and unsocial hours because they are disadvantaged and discriminated against in housing, education and employment. They are consequently less likely than other mothers to send their children to early years settings, such as nursery classes, that are only open for a few hours. As these settings are free, these mothers are disproportionately prevented from using free childcare and education.

Monitoring information reveals practice

Collecting and analysing information to monitor the implementation of practices and procedures helps to reveal discrimination. For example, details about sex, ethnicity and disability can be gathered from people who apply for and are offered a job, or from children who apply for and are offered a place in early years settings.

Other areas of practice and procedure should be monitored for potential forms of discrimination. For example:

- Does everyone have equal chances of promotion and access to training and relevant information?
- Do the resources used – toys, books, jigsaws, dolls and posters – have hidden negative messages?
- Does the building cater for disabilities?
- Do the assessment arrangements give all children an equal chance to succeed, even when they are learning English as an additional language?
- Are the cultures, dialects, accents and languages of all children given equal value?

For detailed consideration of these issues, see Chapter 6.

Prejudice, discrimination and young children

Being treated unfairly is hurtful, but do young children always know when they are being treated unfairly? They certainly know when another child has a bigger portion of pudding or ice cream than they do, but do they react to unfairness in the same way as adults, and do they know when they are treating someone else unfairly?

There are rarely clear answers to these questions but people working with young children and their families need to consider all of them, because concerns around these issues are likely to occur in every form of early years setting at some time or other. They are directly involved in the issue of quality in education and care. Where prejudice and discrimination are present, there cannot be equality, and without equality there cannot be good quality in an early years setting.

On page 10, there are three examples of situations

that might arise in an early years setting. Discriminatory behaviour of the sort shown in each example happens all too frequently in early years practice. Recognising it doesn't mean that an individual adult or child has to be singled out for blame. However, the complexities of the situations and the need to take both an immediate and a long-term approach illustrate that dealing with prejudice and the behaviour resulting from it take time, effort and commitment.

After each example, there is a list of questions focusing on how the children involved might feel and the responses that might be needed from adults and other children. They are questions that people working with young children might stop and ask themselves every day.

All three examples have similarities and differences, but the main principles that should be used to address them are the same.

1 Differences between people should not be linked with ideas of superiority or inferiority.
2 No child or adult should be made to feel unhappy because they are 'different'.
3 While there are real differences between children, and most children have at least one thing they cannot do which most other children can, no child or adult should make another feel unhappy because of these differences.
4 No child or adult should be treated less equally than others because of these differences.
5 All children should be enabled to grow up with positive attitudes to those who are different from themselves as well as those who are similar to themselves.

Asking the right questions

As well as the more obvious expressions of prejudice given in the three examples, there may be occasions where prejudice is hidden from adults unless they watch very carefully. For example, children may whisper remarks or play only with white, able-bodied dolls. But if adults are observant and themselves play with all dolls, prejudice – as opposed to lack of familiarity with the dolls – becomes a more likely explanation for the behaviour.

Young children seldom express prejudice openly. Unless people working with children, parents and family members or carers raise the issue, they will not necessarily know what children are thinking, especially when they do not really want to believe that such young children may be learning to be prejudiced. It cannot be assumed, just because no obvious incidents occur, that young children are not already prejudiced or learning to be so.

What do we mean by prejudice and discrimination? | 9

Example 1

Roger goes to a childminder. His left leg is shorter than his right, so he cannot move very quickly. Josie wants to play hospitals. She asks Altaf to join her and Roger indicates that he would like to play too. Josie says she will be the nurse, Altaf can be the doctor and Roger can be the patient. Roger says he wants to be the doctor but Josie waves him away saying he can't be the doctor 'because of his leg'.

- What might Roger be feeling?
- Why did Josie assume that, because Roger has a particular disability, he cannot play being a doctor?
- What might the childminder or another child say to help Roger not feel hurt?
- How could Josie be helped to understand the effect of what she has said?
- What could the childminder do to ensure that this doesn't happen again?
- What strategy could be developed so that the childminder, children and their families take responsibility to prevent this sort of incident occurring?

Example 2

Alice is at her playgroup playing at making tea in the home corner. Brenda is doing some ironing. Ben comes in and wants to help serve the tea, but both Alice and Brenda shoo him out saying that 'boys aren't allowed' because the mummies are in the kitchen.

- What might Ben be feeling?

- What might a worker or another child have said or done to help him not feel hurt?
- If he was not feeling hurt, what else might he be feeling?
- How could Alice and Brenda be helped to understand the effect of what they did?
- What could workers do to ensure that this doesn't happen again and to help the children have a better understanding of roles?
- What strategy could be developed so that workers, children and their families take responsibility to prevent this sort of incident occurring?

Example 3

The children in the nursery class are playing ring-a-ring-a-roses with their teacher. Felicity, who is four years old and white, refuses to hold Paul's hand. Paul is black. The teacher tries to encourage Felicity to hold Paul's hand but she won't. The teacher holds Paul's hand and afterwards she asks Felicity why she wouldn't hold his hand. Felicity says she doesn't want to because his hand is dirty.

- What might Paul be feeling?
- What might the teacher or another child say or do to make Paul feel less hurt?
- How could Felicity be helped to understand the effect of what she did?
- What could staff do to ensure this does not happen again?
- What strategy could be developed so that the staff, children and their families take responsibility to prevent this sort of incident occurring?

The effect of racism on children

Racism damages all children, black and white, although it does so in different ways. Racism very clearly affects black children and their families, who are greatly disadvantaged by discrimination. For them, racism

- is hurtful and may interfere with their ability to learn;
- may damage their concept of self-identity and/or make them believe that they are seen as inferior outside their homes; and
- can affect their behaviour, their motivation and their confidence.

Black children need to learn that racism is not their fault and is not the result of anything that they have done. It is important to help them establish a positive self image.

Racism also damages white children. It may

- lead them to believe that black people are somehow less human than they are;
- blunt their sensitivity to others and reinforce false notions of their own superiority;
- distort their perceptions of reality by failing to provide them with the full range of information on which they can make their own judgements, for example racism rejects some languages and lifestyles without offering the opportunity of learning about and enjoying them as different;
- lead them to ignore facts or opinions that have been contributed by black people, thus encouraging them to accept partial information as the basis for decision-making; and
- prevent them from learning concepts of empathy to others – concepts that are fundamental to respecting and valuing one another.

10 | Action for racial equality in the early years

There is almost no research on the effects of racism on white children. One piece of research done in the United States in the late 1950s showed that racially prejudiced seven-year-old children were significantly more intolerant of ambiguity than children who were not prejudiced.[2] This means that they jumped to conclusions without testing ideas. They believed their solutions were the only ones possible.

In discussions about 'race', it is usually only black people who are seen as having a racial identity. 'Whiteness', which is part of the racial identity of white people, is rarely acknowledged.

Prejudice, discrimination and adults

The attitudes that people working with young children bring to work can have a significant effect on the early years setting. Whether conscious or not, a hidden agenda may influence practice in favour of some children and away from others. Here are some examples of prejudicial beliefs that people might bring to work, followed by questions that look into their possible consequences:

1 *If you go to live in another country you should adopt the way of life of that country*
   - What effect would this belief have on work with children and families who have migrated to Britain?
   - Would people working with children expect parents to speak only English?
   - Would they expect Muslim children to eat tomato sandwiches from the same plate as ham sandwiches?
   - Would they expect everyone to wear the same sort of clothes?
   - Would they expect all children to join in Christian Christmas prayers?
   - Would they feel the same about all families? For instance, would they feel that French, Japanese, Russian, Bangladeshi and South African families should all adopt the 'British' way of life equally?
   - Would they expect to adopt the German way of life if they went to live in Germany, the Argentinean way of life in Argentina or the Kuwaiti way of life in Kuwait?

2 *Men are more capable of grasping scientific and mathematical concepts than women*
   - What effect might this belief have on science and maths work with girls?

   - Would people working with young children encourage numeracy skills to be learnt more by boys than by girls?
   - Would they praise boys more than girls for completing project work?
   - Would they encourage boys to use computers more than girls?

3 *Working-class children are not as interested in 'learning' as middle-class children*
   - What effect would this have on the time and effort put into helping working-class children develop reading and numeracy skills?
   - Would staff encourage working-class children less than middle-class children?

4 *Deaf children or children learning English as an additional language are not as intelligent as other children* (this may be an unconscious belief)
   - What result would this have on the way adults relate to any of these children?
   - Would they talk to them slowly, loudly or with unnatural emphasis?
   - Could their actions make the children feel awkward and stupid, and perhaps reluctant to speak at all?

It is a good idea if parents and people working with children are provided with opportunities to think carefully about their own attitudes to differences in a non-threatening environment, free of the need to be defensive.

The process of change

It is accepted that what men have learned they can unlearn.[3]

All forms of discrimination must be removed as soon as you become aware of them. People who experience discrimination and prejudice should never be expected to wait until the people who are not experiencing discrimination feel the time is right.

The need for change often represents a difficult balance. There is a conflict between wanting to change things quickly and the knowledge that sudden changes may not last. But changes *are* possible. People *do* change their negative attitudes. Institutions do change their practices and take action to monitor what happens. Structural inequalities *can* be identified and procedures set in place to get rid of them.

But the process of change takes time.

What do we mean by prejudice and discrimination? | **11**

2 | How children learn about racism

A black woman got on a London-bound train in the Cotswolds. She sat at a four-seater table, next to the gangway, beside a little white boy. His mother was sitting opposite him.

Almost immediately the boy started to push and kick the black woman. She asked him why he was pushing her and he said he didn't like her sitting next to him, that he didn't like people like her and he didn't like her hair. His mother noticed what was going on but she did nothing. The black woman told the boy that he didn't have any reason to think anything about her because he didn't know her, but he pushed and kicked her all the more.

Eventually the black woman asked the boy's mother if she could please ask her child to stop what he was doing. The mother replied by saying: 'He's a child, he's only three.' The black woman said she realised that, but as his mother, she was doing nothing to stop him. The mother then said: 'That's the trouble with you people, you've all got chips on your shoulders.'

Imagine an episode where a disabled person, a woman or an older person is subjected to similar behaviour from mother and son.

What specific issues are raised in the example? What may have caused the little boy to behave in this way?

- Was he prejudiced against black people?
- Did his mother say that he was 'only three' because she believed such a young child could not be prejudiced?
- Can such a young child be prejudiced?
- Did the mother think it was all right to treat a black person in this way and, if so, was this because she was prejudiced herself?
- If the little boy was prejudiced, was he born prejudiced?
- Were his actions 'natural' and, if not, where and when might he have learned them?
- Had the boy previously heard his mother making prejudicial remarks? Or had she done nothing when he had heard other remarks or seen prejudiced actions?

Learning to be prejudiced

A group of white three year olds from a nursery in the south London suburbs was on a visit to a museum. On the way, they stopped at the British Rail station in Brixton. As soon as the announcement 'Brixton, this is Brixton' came over the tannoy, the children chorused 'Brixton! We don't like Brixton, do we?'

Where might they have heard of Brixton, in what context, and why had they absorbed negative messages when they are unlikely to have had any personal knowledge or understanding of Brixton?

Children are like sponges. They absorb the attitudes and values of the people around them. Attitudes, including prejudiced attitudes, are not inborn – they are learned, and children learn their attitudes from their whole environment. They learn them from books, dolls, toys and posters, from adults around them, other children and the media, in the following ways.

1 **What children see (and don't see).** If children only see able-bodied people in their books, jigsaw puzzles and posters, they may learn that less able-bodied people are not part of society and have to be kept separate. On television, if children see few women or black people in status roles they may learn to think that only white men can be in these positions in our society.

2 **What children hear (and don't hear).** If a child is with her mum and they meet a friend who refers to 'dirty Pakis', the child may receive the message that it's all right to use the word 'Paki' and that such people are dirty – unless someone immediately explains that the term used by the friend is wrong and completely unacceptable. If no one ever mentions black people and they do not live in the area, children may think that black people do not live anywhere in Britain.

3 **What children do (and don't do).** If a mother won't let her son help in the kitchen but insists her daughter does so, and if their father stresses the 'important' work he is doing on the car with his son, then both children learn that some work is more worthy and of higher status than others.

12 | Action for racial equality in the early years

If Dad never goes in the kitchen, both sons and daughters learn that it is a woman's domain.

From witnessing these sorts of situations, what do children with differing abilities, black children and girls learn about their place in the world, and how might this affect their motivation, their attitudes and their behaviour?

Embarrassed silence

Learned attitudes and values are influenced by the circumstances of the time and passed on from generation to generation, largely unconsciously. Some people may challenge them, others may change them. But because they are often so subtle and hidden, what is really being passed on is often unknown and unacknowledged. So it is only when there is a reason, a focus, for recognising or demonstrating them that they come out into the open.

For example, in a largely white rural area or city suburb, white children and the adults around them may never have seen a black person in the flesh. The sudden appearance of a black person on the street, in the shop or in the early years setting may then provide a forum for dormant racist attitudes to emerge. These attitudes may have been learned from a variety of sources but never actually expressed. Yasmin Alibhai describes an incident she witnessed:

> On the 207 bus the other day, a white toddler filled the lower deck with piercing screams when a black man got on. 'He's black, Mummy, tell him to go away.' We sat throttled with tension as the mother tried to swat the youngster into silence. At some traffic lights, the man obligingly jumped off, the mother said the child was just being silly, and the passengers settled back into the comfort of that statement.[4]

This example reveals the dilemma of what to do in circumstances when no one has ever talked with children about the differences between people. It demonstrates the need to prepare all children, wherever they live, to understand, know about and respect differences at a very early age. It also shows that in any situation – whether public or private – we need to know what action to take with children, with the person who has become the centre of attention (the victim) and with onlookers.

Patricia Williams describes the dilemma of parents having to respond to a child's potentially embarrassing questions in public.[5] In these situations, parents may simply say 'ssssh', but a child is not restrained by manners. By saying 'ssssh', the message given is that there is something odd going on. This may be reinforced when an adult doesn't answer properly or says that the subject is not something to be talked about.

Skin colour

Most four year olds would be expected to tell the difference between a red and a yellow brick and usually to be able to name the colour. So it should not be surprising that they can also recognise skin colour. Even so, there is evidence that some people working with children believe that very young children are incapable of recognising different skin colours, and so they do not prepare for it.

> A setting in a rural area had no toys, jigsaws, dolls or books that included pictures or images of anyone other than white people. When the inspection officer from the local social services department visited, she suggested that they get some more things to reflect today's multicultural British society.
>
> Rather unenthusiastically, particularly because their finances were severely limited, the staff at the setting bought a black doll and a few books with illustrations of black people, and put them with the other things. None of the children played with the doll or chose the books. None of those working with the children played with the doll or read the books or encouraged the children to play with them. One of the workers with the children said: 'There, I knew it would be a waste of money to buy that sort of stuff for here.'
>
> Soon after, Sunita, who is three and whose parents came to Britain from India, joined the group. On her second day Charlene who's four and white, laughed at Sunita when she talked in Hindi and said she didn't like her because her face was 'ugly, pooey brown'. The same worker who had complained about wasting money said 'That's not nice' and distracted Charlene from saying more. She suggested to Sunita that she should take no notice.
>
> The worker recounted the incident to one of the others, who agreed the incident must simply have been a clash of personalities as 'children don't really notice colour'. They decided to try to get Charlene to make friends with Sunita.

How children learn about racism | **13**

The two workers allowed their existing ideas to rule out the chance that Charlene was prejudiced against Sunita on grounds of skin colour. Their superficial response to the incident left Sunita to experience her hurt alone and Charlene with no clear idea of exactly what was wrong with her comment and her laughter.

Could the failure to acknowledge colour as an issue be due to the fact that white people seldom mention skin colour differences to each other because, somehow, it is considered rude to draw attention to such differences? Or might they believe the child is unfortunate to have a black skin, so they don't want to draw attention to it?

Perhaps what people actually believe is that skin colour differences are not important to young children – that children really don't see them. This is not supported by facts, as when children are asked specifically about skin colours they can usually describe them accurately.

What children do pick up from adults is the message that skin colour is an issue that they shouldn't talk about. This indicates the importance of discussing differences with children in a positive way – rather than keeping a silence that reflects negative attitudes – and of working with families to raise issues at home as well as in early years settings.

Where young children have been given positive messages about the range of people's skin colours, they feel free to talk about them in the same way as they talk about other things. Unlike many other children and adults they feel able to say what they think. And they do.

Ramiz, aged three, whose mother is of mixed-race parentage, was sitting with his maternal grandmother at breakfast. When she asked him what kind of sugar he wanted on his cereal. Ramiz said: 'I'll have brown sugar because I'm brown, and you have white sugar because you're white.'

Skin colour is very important to children, and adults should never indicate that a child's skin colour 'doesn't matter'. This simply ignores the reality of racism.

Racial attitudes

Research from Britain, the United States, New Zealand and Australia has provided evidence that children as young as two or three years old notice racial differences.[6] Two researchers found that the failure to recognise children's 'blackness' damaged some black children's view of themselves and that children's racial identity is crucial for their successful development.[7]

The research shows that as soon as children are able to express what they are thinking, most of them associate negative or positive attitudes with racial differences – unless specific action to the contrary had been taken by those responsible for them. Young children were racialised before they went to primary school.

Using black and white dolls as images of black and white people, the research shows that white children as young as three or four years old were much more likely to prefer white dolls than black children were to prefer black dolls. Many of the white children showed a degree of hostility towards the black dolls. It is difficult to assess the true racial attitudes of young children, and using dolls is not an accurate test because they do not represent real people. Nevertheless, the choices made by the children in this research probably reflect the attitudes they met in their environments. They were learning to hold racist attitudes and beliefs. From the day they are born, young white children are learning the beginnings of racial and often racist attitudes – just as they are learning the beginnings of language.

What little evidence there is shows that young black children are much less likely to display negative racial attitudes.

Living in mainly 'white' areas

I run a playgroup in the country so it's not a problem for us. We haven't any of 'them' here.
Playgroup leader in a rural area

In Britain today there are very few areas that could genuinely be described as 'white'. Most areas have some black people living and working in them, and even in a county like Cornwall one per cent of the population is black or from a minority ethnic community.

There is considerable evidence that black people in rural areas suffer from racism as much as in urban areas, but the impact is often different. Many teachers and even carers will deny that name-calling happens, and black children living in these places often suffer in silence. The reason that many people say there is no issue of racism in white areas may be because there are no – or few – black people living there. The racist attitudes are lying dormant and stay there until black people come to live there.

One report describes the racist abuse experienced by Asian primary school children in Norwich, but no one appeared to take it seriously. It was either not seen as a problem or not seen as a racial one.[8] Two more recent reports vividly describe the extent of racism in rural, largely white areas – southwest England[9] and Norfolk.[10]

Even the BBC's radio programme *Farming today* produced a whole edition on 'rural racism'.[11] It referred to a headteacher who said that there had been no trouble with racism until M (a young black boy) came to his school. What he should have said is that no one noticed that racism existed in the area until M arrived.

It is obvious, really, that if there is no one present to be the 'victim' of racist attitudes, then it will appear that racism does not exist. No one has heard anyone say anything racist to anyone or seen anyone do anything racist – unless they have seen it on television or read about it.

Without any positive messages about racial differences, the slightest 'indications' of racism may be all that young white children hear or see about the issue. These slight indications build up to form their attitudes. For example, the occasional or rare racist remark about black or minority ethnic people only has to be said once or twice in a child's hearing for the principle to be absorbed ('Well, Dad doesn't like them'). If the remark is more specific, what may be learned is that 'they smell', 'they are dirty' or 'they should go back to their own country'.

A four-year old white girl living in the north of Scotland, with no black families in the vicinity, was visited by her aunt, also white, and her friend, a black Nigerian man. When she saw the Nigerian man, the little girl asked if he was a boxer. He said he wasn't. She then said: 'Well you must have been in prison then!'

The girl had learned something about black people from somewhere, even if she had not actually met a black person before. It was only the man's physical presence that provided a stimulus for her to express her idea. If he had not been there she might never have said anything to demonstrate her thoughts – her family and carers might never have known what she thought, or believed her capable of such thoughts. Children are learning to make sense of the world around them – and in some cases they are learning to be racially prejudiced right under our noses, whether or not we have noticed it happening.

Those working with young children in white areas should not fool themselves into thinking that there is no 'problem' there. If anything, the work to be done is even more important in order to:

- give children a chance not to be influenced by racism;
- prepare them for living in a multiracial society;
- help them unlearn any notions of white superiority that they have already learned; and
- give them the skills to challenge inequality for themselves.

If the situation is allowed to continue unaltered, nothing will change. The cycle of learning racist attitudes will continue and discrimination will be maintained.

3 | Talking about racism

At last there is a real understanding of race, and the ancient and disreputable idea that the peoples of the world are divided into biologically distinct units has gone forever.[12]

Many white people find it difficult to find the words for discussing racial issues. Sometimes they are afraid of using particular words for fear of offending someone and saying something that is apparently, but not intentionally, rude. Faced with the issue of a person's racial group or ethnicity, some white people may deal with it by trying to avoid using any specific words at all. This may be because they do not know many black people personally or do not feel comfortable enough to discuss such things with them.

Different people, whether black or white, make a variety of choices as to which terms they like to use to describe themselves and others. Clearly some are unacceptable and are largely recognised as such. Others are the topic of differing opinions and, because of this, such differences cannot easily be resolved. It is important to understand that the use of any racial term involves strongly held beliefs and feelings. There is consequently a need to be sensitive and adaptable.

It is easier to raise issues and ask questions if an atmosphere of trust and respect between people has been built up. In this situation it becomes more comfortable to 'correct' or discuss particular terminology without giving offence or being offended. Constant, open discussion generally makes it easier to ask people what they wish to be called and which words they prefer to use when talking about 'race'.

Meanings can change

Terminology changes with time. What might be acceptable to some people one day may, in a very short time, be less acceptable or unacceptable. For example, the term 'coloured' has been used by white (and sometimes by black) people in the past to describe others and themselves. It is still used by some older people now, often because they feel it is rude to describe someone as 'black'. The fact that the word 'coloured' is considered more 'polite'

by many of the people who use it shows that it was not always seen as a negative term by everyone. However, it has a significant association with colonialism, slavery and apartheid that has made it come to be seen as a negative term, and it is not used so frequently now.

Other terms are racially offensive at all times and have always been seen as such by the recipient. Terms such as 'Nigger', 'Wop', 'Coon', 'Gyppo', 'Wog', 'Yid', 'Dago', 'Paki', 'Kike' and 'Paddy' were and are racist in intent and hurtful to the recipient. They are unacceptable.

The terms 'Caucasian', 'Negroid' and 'Mongoloid' derive from attempts to categorise people according to their skin colour and physical characteristics. There is no scientific basis for these divisions and they have no place in Britain today.

Words used for talking about racism

The terminology used in this book applies to Britain. It may or may not be applicable elsewhere. Care should always be taken when using terminology in non-British contexts. Terms that are obvious to us may have a completely different meaning for people in other communities.

Describing people

Words are constantly changing in their use and acceptability. Here are some words and how they are commonly used:

- **African-Caribbean:** People whose origins are from Africa and/or the Caribbean.
- **Asian and South Asian:** People from, or originating from, India, Bangladesh, Pakistan and Sri Lanka.
- **black, Black:** People who are discriminated against because of their skin colour. These words are usually used as 'political' terms, to unite the people who are discriminated against. Some people use the term 'Black' to refer specifically to people of African-Caribbean origin.
- **Ethnic minority, ethnic majority:** People whose ethnic group is in a minority or majority in a country. It includes people of all skin colours.

16 | Action for racial equality in the early years

- **Minority ethnic, majority ethnic:** These terms are often preferred to the two above as they recognise that everyone has an ethnicity, whether it is in the majority or the minority.
- **Mixed parentage, mixed 'race', mixed heritage:** People whose parents are from different ethnic or racial groups. Sometimes there is a conflict between what people feel themselves to be and how others may perceive them, which may lead to particularly strong views about terminology. It is important to listen to and respect what is being said and felt. (The term 'half-caste' has fallen out of use in much the same way as the term 'coloured', but for different reasons. It is a negative term suggesting that a person doesn't really fit in anywhere.)
- **Travellers:** People who are traditionally nomadic, whether they are still so or not. If they are nomadic they move around, but the majority now live in houses or on permanent sites, while still being Travellers. Even when Travellers live in houses, they may travel in the summer. They still experience racism.

  Nomadic Travellers travel from place to place seeking work but, because most of their original work is no longer in demand, they have adapted to other trades. They include English and Welsh Gypsies (some of whom may be Romany Gypsies), fairground and circus people, Irish and Scottish Travellers (who sometimes call themselves Gypsies), Bargees and New Travellers (who are generally seeking an alternative way of life) and, more recently, European Roma who have obtained refugee or immigrant status.

  The term 'Traveller' has a capital 'T' ('travellers' would include tourists and commercial travellers). The term 'Gypsy' has a capital 'G' (see section on Travellers and itinerant communities on pages 36–37 for further details).
- **white, White:** This is again a political term. It refers to people who are not 'black' and who are usually of European origin, whose skin colour or tone is pale.
- People from countries such as China, Vietnam, Nagaland, Italy, Cyprus, Egypt and those in eastern Europe do not fit into any of the above categories. They may simply be described as coming from that country. Note that countries such as South Africa, Ghana and Egypt all belong to the continent of Africa.

Everyone can make mistakes. What is needed is the confidence to become familiar with these words and to use them as part of a commitment to remove racism, by talking about them in an atmosphere of trust and by not being afraid to make a mistake and learn from it.

Other terms

As with the previous group of words, some of the following may change their interpretation over time.

- **Anti-racist, anti-racism** refers to resources, policies, practices and procedures that recognise the existence of racism in its many forms and take appropriate action to remove it. Anti-racism recognises racism as being the major obstacle to racial equality.
- **Anti-Semitism** is racism against Jewish people.
- **Culture** Everyone has a 'culture' as a result of their lives and experiences. It includes all those factors that have contributed to these experiences. It is not just the 'high days' and festivals but also the minutiae of everyday life. Elements of culture may include factors such as language, social class, religious beliefs and practices, 'traditions', dress and food. No culture is superior or inferior to another.
- **Ethnic data** (for example, information about the ethnic composition of the local community) is collected in various ways, according to the reason for collecting it. There should always be a clear reason for collecting ethnic data, including an explanation for why it is needed and what will be done with it, plus a clear statement of confidentiality (that the identity of individuals surveyed will not be available).
- **Ethnicity** refers to an individual's identification with a group sharing some or all of the same culture, lifestyle, language, religion, nationality, geographical region and history. Every person has an ethnicity. Concepts of 'ethnic food', 'ethnic dress' and 'ethnic books' are therefore nonsense.
- **Ethnocentrism** is the process of viewing or interpreting the world from the perspective of a particular ethnic group. 'Eurocentrism' is, for example, viewing the non-European world from a European perspective.
- **Multiculturalism** is an acceptance and positive attitude towards the cultural variety in society. However, multiculturalism may simply provide ammunition to reinforce racism unless there is recognition of the way that different cultures are ranked in a racial hierarchy (see page 25 for further discussion).
- **Non-racist** refers to resources, policies, practices and procedures that take a neutral approach to racism, neither acknowledging it, denying it nor opposing it.
- **'Race'** is in everyday use, but the word 'race' is in quotation marks here because it is a controversial term. The word comes from historical attempts to categorise people according to their skin colour and physical characteristics. There is no scientific basis for

Talking about racism | **17**

divisions into biologically determined groups. Individuals, not nations or 'races', are the main sources of human variation.

- **Racial discrimination** is the treatment of people of some 'races' less favourably than others would be treated in the same circumstances. Under the 1976 Race Relations Act racial discrimination is defined specifically, in several ways, to cover particular situations and circumstances.

- **Racial group** refers to those who are of, or belong to, the same 'race'. They have the same racial origins.

- **Racial harassment** refers to verbal, non-verbal or physical aggression towards people of various 'races'. If the 'victim' believes that it was because they belong to a particular racial group then, unless proved otherwise, it is usually defined as 'racial' harassment, whatever other people may say. In some situations children may not realise they are being racially harassed or abused, but adults who witness the incident will be able to identify it.

- **Racial prejudice** is the term for opinion or attitude about people of various 'races', based on false or inadequate evidence. It is a tendency to judge people in a particular way and is often self-perpetuating because the (usually negative) judgement of people from different 'races' prevents any interaction with them. Surveys in Britain show that white people are more likely to be racially prejudiced than others. However, racial prejudice may exist (and sometimes does) between any racial groups. Racial prejudice, where some groups are marked out as 'different', is found in most parts of the world.

- **Racial stereotyping** is categorisation (usually negative) of a whole racial group of people because of the actions or behaviour of one person, or a few people, or as the result of racial prejudice. It is also when a general stereotype is transferred to a particular person. It often becomes part of the cultural legacy. It is still stereotyping even if the stereotype is positive – for example, being 'good at sport', 'having a sense of rhythm' or 'having the gift of the gab' are all racial stereotypes when applied to groups of people.

- **Racism** is all practices and procedures that discriminate against people because of their colour, culture and/or 'race' or ethnicity. It includes the whole package of racial prejudice, discrimination, stereotyping, making racist assumptions, harassment, institutional and structural racism and ethnocentrism. In Britain there is racism against Jewish people, Asian people, Chinese people, Irish people, Travellers, black people, Gypsies, people from many other ethnic groups, people from particular nationalities and often refugees and asylum seekers. So many social, economic and political decisions are in the hands of white people and have been so historically, that white people rarely suffer from institutional and structural forms of racial discrimination in Britain.

  - *Institutional racism* is racism that is not usually a result of an individual action, and works in precisely the same way as institutional discrimination (see definition on page 8) to discriminate against people specifically because of their 'race'. Such practices and procedures are often long established, but have failed to take account of the reality of multiracial Britain. This is similar to 'indirect racial discrimination', as defined under the 1976 Race Relations Act.

  - *Structural racism* is racism that is not a result of individual action or of an institutional nature, where the existing structures of the society discriminates against particular racial groups.

What these terms really mean

The terms given on pages 16–18 are definitions and may have different meanings or be used differently when applied to real life.

No terms are agreed by everyone. The contradictions and conflicts that the use of many terms arouse in people must be acknowledged, even if they are not all understood. Very few terms are set in stone, fixed in meaning for ever. The continual changes in word meanings and interpretations, and the need to explore the issues around words, reflect the fact that the debate about 'race' and culture is ongoing. It will always be so.

Black, black

The word 'black' is often misused. It was first used in Britain in the 1960s, when people of many different ethnic origins, but with a skin colour that was not 'white', wanted a term to describe themselves in order that they could present a more united front against the racism they all experienced. 'Black' seemed the most acceptable word and it is a political term.

In the past, the word 'black' was often used negatively and offensively. In the United States during the 1960s, there was a huge campaign to reclaim the word positively and particularly to stress the idea that 'Black is beautiful'. Most white people at that time saw black people as inevitably ugly (this was tied to white people's own perceptions of superiority), so it was a vitally important campaign

18 | Action for racial equality in the early years

to make people rethink their ideas and accept that 'beauty is in the eye of the beholder' and not the sole right of white people. The concept of what is beautiful is learned, so it can be unlearned.

Everyone needs to be aware of the large number of negative ways that the word 'black' can be used and the number of positive ways that white is used. For example, 'pure white gloves', 'dirty black hands' and 'black mark'. For a child to have his hands described as 'dirty black' may reinforce black as being a dirty colour by definition. It is, therefore, likely to be hurtful. It also reinforces, in the ears of white children, the negative association of black and dirty – as if they go together.

However, a lot of nonsense has been written and said about using the word 'black'. In the 1980s, sections of the media and others cooked up stories about various anti-racist organisations and local authorities, allegedly saying that they had banned terms like 'black coffee' or 'black bin liner' because they would be offensive to black people. These stories were without foundation and were used to ridicule the organisations, making them appear to be extreme forms of thought police.

There are many words and phrases such as 'blackboard', 'white snow' and 'black bin liner' that are accurate descriptions and which make no value judgements, either positive or negative. It is absolutely appropriate for these things to be defined in this way. A sensitivity and a sense of reality are needed here.

Culture

The word 'culture' is often used only to describe the culture of people who are not white.

When white English people are asked to describe their culture, they usually find it difficult and may end up talking about top hats, roast beef, rolled umbrellas, Beefeaters and Morris dancing. They then realise that these things are not typical of the majority of English people. Similarly, most French people's culture does not include carrying strings of onions and not all Mexicans wear sombreros.

Cultural stereotyping is not only ridiculous, it is dangerous, because it makes assumptions that do not reflect reality. Everyone has a culture, or cultures, but it seems that only *some* people are required to define what their culture means for them. Most white English people just take whatever is their culture for granted and find it difficult to define in precise terms, whereas other white British

people – the Welsh, Scottish, Irish and Cornish – can clearly talk about their own distinctive cultures. Usually, only people who migrate to Britain are 'required' to describe their cultures so that they can be analysed, evaluated and accepted – or not. It is as if white (English) culture is hardly a culture at all, it is simply taken as the norm by which every other culture is judged.

Ethnicity

There are links between culture and ethnicity, but ethnicity is more specific in its geographical origin. For example, people born in Delhi in India have a Delhi (Indian) ethnic origin, wherever they move to. The same person's culture might change over time, particularly after emigration. Aspects of the culture may change but the ethnicity remains the same.

Minority ethnic or ethnic minority people are frequently and incorrectly called 'ethnics'. In Britain they usually have brown or black skin colours and the words often take on the same meaning (ie, ethnic minority *equals* ethnic *equals* brown or black). Used in this way, the term 'ethnic minority' becomes a descriptive term rather than a term describing a proportion of people.

Talking the same language

It takes a long time before specific meanings for terms are understood by everyone and used equally by them. Difficulties involved in coming to a common understanding are revealed when people from different countries with different histories and understandings of the world try to work together using a common language. For example, a recent European seminar looking at racism in childcare and education was held in England. Early on, one of the participants said she was unable to continue working in a racist hotel (the venue for the seminar). She showed the others a sign in the foyer saying 'Only residents may use the lounge'. She had understood 'resident' to mean 'citizen'.

Another misunderstanding is where words are translated literally. For example, at an international conference for childminders the term black childminder' was initially used interchangeably with 'illegal' or 'unofficial' childminder, as in black market.

The English language is forever changing. The important point when using and discussing words for talking about 'race' is to be continually receptive and sensitive to the words that other people use and their reactions to yours.

4 | Learning from the past

When assessing the developmental progress of children, it is important to have some standards, or norms, by which each child can be measured on a range of factors. Children who are genuinely developmentally delayed need to be identified as early as possible in order to address the causes of the delay.

Until very recently most of these norms were devised using white, middle-class children as the basis. Some norms apply to all children, but others depend on the particular group which is being assessed. Different child-rearing practices and environments may result in different norms being applicable. In most cases one type of practice is neither better nor worse than another – they are just different. For example, a child's ability to hold a pencil or a paintbrush will clearly relate to their experience. Some young Chinese children may have especially well-developed painting skills as a result of their experience of their cultural heritage.

Culturally biased tests may lead to inaccurate assessments. It is important therefore, when assessing a child's development, that differences of upbringing and environment are taken into account. During developmental tests in the 1980s the following incidents took place:

Test: Recognises common animals

A four-year-old Muslim boy was shown pictures of several farm animals, including a pig, and asked to name them. He named all except the pig correctly, but expressed apprehension at the pig's picture and showed extreme reluctance to name it.

A Muslim nursery assistant, who happened to pass by as the test was being conducted, explained to the tester how inappropriate and insensitive the question was, as Muslim children are taught not to say the word for pig in their language (which, for example, may be Urdu, Arabic or Punjabi). It is seen as an obscenity. Any question that asked a child to name a pig would therefore inevitably fail to assess a Muslim child's full knowledge of animal recognition.

Test: Uses a knife and fork competently

An four-year-old Indian girl was given a knife and fork and a plate, and was asked to show how she used them to eat her dinner. She stared blankly and clearly did not know what to do with the knife and fork.

It turned out that in this child's home, knives were kept in a special drawer and used only by her mother when preparing food. The family always ate their dinner with their fingers, so the girl could not possibly demonstrate how to eat dinner with a knife and fork.

Despite being able to hold a pencil 'competently' and to do up her buttons, this child was incorrectly assessed by the knife and fork test because the manipulative skills she had were not assessed on this occasion.

Neither of these children was developmentally delayed, but aspects of the tests were inappropriate to their particular cultural experiences. The use of these and similar tests might have resulted in groups of children being assessed incorrectly, at least in part. Some testing checklists still include 'the ability to use a knife and fork', regardless of a child's cultural experiences.

The language of the test and the language of the assessor may make it impossible to accurately assess children who are learning English as an additional language but who have not yet acquired the vocabulary to understand and answer the questions as well as they could in their home language. This may result in underestimating their knowledge.

This issue is of particular importance when considering the practices and procedures for baseline assessment. Young children who are learning English should not be assessed by people who can only speak English using a test drafted in English. Such an assessment is insufficient and unacceptable.

20 | Action for racial equality in the early years

Books and research on child development

Until the late 1980s, books written about child development and child-rearing practices rarely credited the presence of people from a range of social groups. They largely ignored black people and others from minority ethnic groups. If books did take account of them, it was mainly to see them as posing 'problems'.

When researchers started to consider black and minority ethnic children and their families, the messages that emerged were mostly negative and stereotypical. They failed to acknowledge the existence of racism and its possible effect on the development of young children and the interpretation of their behaviour. Nor did they make any attempt to examine the effects of racism on white children.

For example, a particularly influential book for nursery nurse students in the early 1980s was *Child care and health for nursery nurses*. It had this to say:

> *West Indian children may appear to have a 'different' emotional make-up, and will cry and fight, laugh and love with equal energy. Their responsiveness to music makes it almost impossible for them to remain still when music is being played ... Asian children may appear very passive and dependent on adults, as they are encouraged to be dependent and obedient within their families.*[13]

Such statements could have led students to allow black boys to dominate physical activities while giving them less access to cognitive learning skills than other children (see the example of Joe and Rita on page 7).

Other books and research publications drew false conclusions about families and parenting practices. For example, research conducted in Brixton, south London, to measure 'West Indian' children's development, concluded that they fell below the standard of white, urban working-class children in being disproportionately non-verbal in their communication, deaf, showing autistic behaviour and with poor motor skills.[14]

In the same year Greta Sandler, a playbus organiser in Lewisham, also in south London, wrote to the Community Relations Commission (now the Commission for Racial Equality) at their request stating her concerns about young black children.[15] She was unaware of the Brixton research and its findings. From her observations, she said that many of the children were coming to the playbus and to nurseries in an environment that failed to take account of the reality of their lives, thus making it

appear hostile to them. Many were traumatised by their experiences and their lives were seen by many white workers to be the result of deficient models of parenting. Sandler claimed that, like many other migrant children, they appeared withdrawn and sometimes mute. There were very few resources to reflect their cultural experiences and help them build their identities, and the fact that they were black was rarely taken into account. When a black worker was employed on the playbus, the children responded positively to their presence.

Taken alongside the Brixton research, Sandler's comments go a long way to explain its findings. In Brixton, the children were assessed with little account taken of the fact that they were black that few resources reflected their culture, that they were environmentally and financially disproportionately disadvantaged and that they were likely to have experienced racism. Using standards developed to measure the white English culture, their mothers were described as 'inadequate' and 'unmotherly'. However, the research failed to discover from the parents what behaviour they used to express their love and caring for their children, nor how they saw childhood and guided their children's development according to their values. In the absence of such evidence, conclusions cannot be drawn about parenting practices. Another piece of research in the 1970s identified the disproportionate number of 'West Indian' children being classified as 'subnormal' in schools.[16]

Sandler voiced her concern that black children were being labelled. Research showing that black children fell disproportionately below the developmental standards of white children was leading to black children being disproportionately assessed as priority cases for places in social services day nurseries. Later research proved this to be true.[17] This, in turn, led to black families being thought of as problematic and at risk', so many nursery workers came to see their place of work as a child protection environment.

Stereotyping and labelling had long-term effects on attitudes to child development, the consequences of which may still exist today.

In the absence of any reference to our multicultural, multiracial society in most work published before the 1980s, anything that did address it, however inaccurately, assumed an undeserved authority. For example training courses, particularly for nursery nurses, widely used *Child care and health for nursery nurses*, despite its limitations (see left). It was only in 1989 that the Equal Opportunities Working Party of the National Nursery Examination Board (NNEB) advised tutors that the book did not

Learning from the past | 21

comply with the board's equal opportunities policy. To its credit the NNEB wrote a detailed critique of the book citing all its many examples of racism.

In 1991, the Working Group Against Racism in Children's Resources published guidelines about selecting and evaluating books on child development that addressed racism and its effect.[18] It drew attention to the need to examine the issues critically from an anti-racist perspective, to ensure that books reflect accurately the reality of British society and to consider what is 'normal development' in such a context.

The 1990s have seen the publication of more positive books in this field. It is therefore important to consider not only the content of books but also to take into account the publication date. However, the text must not be *assumed* to address racism effectively just because it has been published recently. When evaluating books, it may be helpful to look up key words in the index and read the relevant text. For example, look for terms like racism, 'race', 'race' relations, equality, equal opportunities, discrimination, attitudes and ethnicity.

The role of the media

During the 1990s the media in general, and television in particular, made great strides in showing a more representative view of our multiracial society. All young children can at least see some visual representations of people like themselves. However, newspapers lag behind this progress in terms of addressing racism in the early years in positive ways.

The purpose of newspapers is generally to tell readers something they don't know and there is great competition to tell the most interesting 'story'. Newspapers rarely take a genuine interest in either young children (except where they abuse, are abused or are perceived as having or being 'problems') or those who work with them. They often seem to have little regard for the consequences of what they write or say.

During the 1980s the tabloid newspapers and some of the broadsheets were at the forefront of attacking the so-called 'loony left'. Everyone, of any political persuasion, who tried to address racism in education seriously was lumped together and labelled as a 'trouble-maker' or as a 'race spy'. The media largely failed to support those who were trying to raise issues of racism in terms of the needs of both black and white children.

Emotive words like 'toddler', 'innocence', 'indoctrination' and 'censorship' were used to draw attention to the work that people were trying to do with young children. They implied that these people were causing trouble where none existed before and that if they would leave things alone everything would be all right. For example, a story, allegedly originating from an Islington playgroup, was circulated. It said that the local council had decreed that the nursery rhyme 'Baa baa black sheep' must no longer be used unless it was changed to 'Baa baa green sheep'. This was not true. Nevertheless the story turned up in many parts of the country and is still floating around. A media group in the Department of Communications at the University of London's Goldsmiths' College monitored the bizarre progress of this 'story' over a period of several years, and published their findings in 1987.

Another example concerned a tabloid which, on hearing that a home counties education authority had introduced a policy on racial harassment as a result of wide consultation, questioned an education officer of the council. He said that even children as young as four could be racially prejudiced and the next day there appeared in large bold letters, on the front page of the paper – 'Racist check on toddlers'.[19] It was followed up the day afterwards by a feature article and an article in a London evening paper.

Today, although a few journals such as *Nursery World* have frequent features on young children and racial issues, articles and news elsewhere are rare. Occasionally, an ill-informed feature still appears. For example in 1996, *The Daily Telegraph* ran a full-page article ridiculing the 'multi-ethnic muddle in our nurseries' and implying that 'British children' are being denied their 'Britishness'. The reporter failed to acknowledge the existence of racist attitudes and behaviour in our society. She also belittled genuine attempts by nursery staff to counter racism by providing positive resources.[20]

Language

All that a child needs for the successful development of language is access to language.[21]

There are 10,000 living languages in the world. Multilingualism is normal.[22]

It has long been accepted that all children living in Britain need to learn standard English so that they can function effectively in our society. But interacting with other English-speaking children has not always been recognised as one of the best ways for children to learn English as an additional language.

Knowledge about other languages has often been limited too. Some people believed that 'African',

22 | Action for racial equality in the early years

'Indian', 'Islamic' and 'Pakistani' were genuine languages. This led to situations where the issue of exactly what language a child spoke was not felt to be important. Children were sometimes reluctant to speak with their parents in their home language when people who worked with them were present. This perhaps indicated that the language was not felt by the child to be valued in the setting. Even very young children can feel the pressure of their peers and adults to conform.

Until quite recently, when children (or adults) spoke together in a language that others could not understand, many adults would feel uncomfortable. Perhaps they thought they were being talked about. Perhaps they felt excluded and powerless because they could not understand, and so interpreted the behaviour as rude. They might also have thought that children should not be 'allowed' to speak their home language in an early years setting. Apart from feeling a lack of control over the situation they saw it as preventing the children from learning to communicate in English, though there is no scientific evidence that this is true.

It was believed in Britain that bilingual children would not be as fluent in either of their languages as children who spoke only one language. In fact the vast majority of the world's people speak more than one language. It is well established that learning to be bilingual or multilingual is an asset, not a disadvantage, when learning English or any other language. The skills needed for one language, for example knowledge of grammar, can be transferred when learning another, however different they may seem.

Research shows that where people working with children value their home languages, the children's ability in other languages flourishes.[23] However, this is not always acknowledged, as the following example from 1997 shows.

An early years setting had several Asian children who spoke various Asian languages at home. They were only allowed to speak English in the setting. An Asian helper, speaking three Asian languages, was also forbidden to speak anything apart from English. The Ofsted nursery inspector explained that refusal to allow any other languages in the setting was not in the best interests of the children learning English, but those in charge said they believed what they were doing was right.

Learning a few or more words of a language that children speak is a solid gesture of support and welcome to children and their families. And it can be fun. It is important to teach children basic words like 'Hello' in a variety of languages and to build links with parents and families where there is no common language. A recognition that some families will not be able to read or understand English can be put into practice by translating and interpreting, according to people's needs.

Four-year-old Delroy laughed at Yasmin when she spoke in Gujerati. Susie, who is nearly five, touched Delroy's arm lightly and said: 'She's clever. She can speak English as well.'

Are some languages more important than others?

Languages are often perceived in a racial hierarchy – with some being more valued than others. For example in Britain, French and Spanish are generally considered more 'useful' than Urdu or Arabic.

Where young children become aware of this – and they learn very quickly whether their home language is accepted, ignored or even laughed at – it can interfere with their learning of English. A person's home language is central to their sense of self, and laughing at a child's language or accent is effectively an assault on who they are and what they stand for. It is likely to be the most powerful deterrent to speaking the language in front of others again, but also interferes in their confidence for learning English – the very thing that everyone wants them to be able to do. A similar result is likely to occur if those working with young children virtually ignore the fact that they are fluent in a language other than English. It is the positive and active valuing of a child's first language that facilitates the process of learning English most effectively.

Some languages are wrongly devalued because they do not have a written form. Others, such as Creole, are often seen as 'incorrect' forms of English. But Creole is a separate language with its own grammatical structure.

In places where people are illiterate, there is often a strong oral culture. To communicate successfully in these communities, oral methods need to be developed and used. For example, the use of video and tapes with Travellers may help families understand the value of early years education. It may give them confidence to know that their children will be respected and valued in an early years setting.

Learning from the past | **23**

In the past, the devaluing of languages meant that some children who were just beginning to learn English, were referred to as 'having no language' or 'not speaking'. Clearly, almost every child has a language and speaks it. Language is a fundamental aspect of a child's personal and cultural identity.

What's so good about English?

It is important to realise that English has no linguistic advantage over any other language or dialect.

Every language has an equal ability to express human needs and ideas and any language can grow to include new words for new ideas. They all have rules for making words and for the way sentences are put together. There are no 'primitive' languages.

Complex ideas can be expressed in all languages. Some have a greater number of words than others to describe something of critical importance to them. For example, the Inuit have a large number of words for different kinds of snow because it plays such a significant role in their lives, while Arabs and Bedouins have many words for camels, and computer whizzkids have lots of terms for computer software.

English is now recognised as the language of the world, but this is not because it has any innate linguistic advantages – it is because English is the language of power in a world dominated by English-speaking peoples. This reinforces any notions of linguistic superiority held by white English people. Although more and more white English people now speak other languages, it is still far from the norm for them to do so.

Everyone who speaks English does so with an accent, whether they are from Newcastle, Pakistan, Ghana or China, and whether they live in a Wolverhampton semi-detached or in Buckingham Palace. Of course, it is important for everyone speaking English to be understood by other English-speaking people, but do white English people make an equal effort to understand people speaking different English accents? Do they listen to and hear what is being said in an Indian or Nigerian accent in the same way as they listen to and hear a Glaswegian accent? And, if someone is difficult to understand, is the situation addressed or is lack of understanding blamed on 'foreignness'?

Many families, not only minority ethnic families, have members who speak languages other than English. Early years settings that take advantage of this diversity and put into practice this living experience encourage everyone to feel welcome and valued. For those families learning English as an additional language, welcoming words in their home language goes a long way to helping the children, parents and those working with the children feel comfortable together. Where people working with children learning English also speak the home language of the children, there is an even greater feeling of security and understanding.

Words and pictures

Words, pictures and their associations often remain deep in our memories long after they have ceased to be commonly used. Dictionary definitions of words do not always accurately define or describe what they have come to mean in everyday usage. For example, in Britain the word 'civilised' – while not defined on racial grounds – is not usually associated with people of non-European origin. It has become 'loaded' with connotations of what people with European origin are, even though the oldest of the world's 'civilisations' were non-European (for example the Egyptians and the Persians).

On the other hand, the word 'primitive' conjures up in the minds of many white people images of black people, living in mud huts, wearing grass skirts, often with painted faces and bodies, and performing 'strange' rituals. The origins of this mythical imagery come partly from films and picture books that were printed earlier this century. Many of them are still around – the Tarzan movies are still shown on TV, sometimes during school holidays – and they reinforce stereotypes that go largely unchallenged, perhaps because people have no experience of the reality of Africa and perhaps because they feel no personal need to challenge them.

Terms associated with visual images can be very powerful on young minds. Words such as 'jungle', 'savages', 'war-dance' and 'cannibal' need to be carefully considered before they are used as they may be associated negatively with and used incorrectly to describe particular groups of people.

Other words in common usage may imply meanings that need to be questioned. For example, the words 'correct', 'proper' and 'suitable' may, in some circumstances, express subjective personal opinions and not matters of fact. Is there a 'correct' way of speaking, for example, and what is meant by a 'suitable' way to dress?

White, English history and stereotypes sometimes distort perceptions of reality. For example, there are skyscrapers, glass-fronted offices and big hotels in most African countries, but how many white people would picture this in their mind's eye? People live in various types of homes according to their needs, their economic situations, the weather and the environment – but are these measured in terms of an English perception of what is 'proper'?

24 | Action for racial equality in the early years

Many white people's images of Africa, specifically of West and East Africa, are wildly out of touch with the truth. If a 'tribal' dance from Zambia is seen on television, performed for a particular special visitor, it may be no more 'typical' of Zambia than Morris dancing is of England.

The vast majority of people seen in the media – in newspapers and magazines, and on TV – are white. Although there was a significant improvement during the 1990s, children are still rarely presented with positive role models of black people in positions of authority. That is why it is important to have stories and picture books portraying a range of people in a variety of roles, chosen with care and with a critical eye to the messages being given by the illustrations.

Multiculturalism

Most white people working with young children in the 1960s and 1970s saw African-Caribbean, Asian and other minority ethnic children as needing to assimilate into the rest of the community, for their own sakes. This meant that they had to change to fit into their new environment but no one else had to change the way they behaved. Two factors prevented people from assimilating:

- people who move to live in another country seldom give up aspects of their own culture in order to 'assimilate'; and
- racism in society generally made it impossible for them to assimilate, even if they wanted to.

Inner city areas, where most black families lived, were often seen by experts as areas of social need. This was probably partly a result of the Plowden Report on primary school children, which identified social deprivation as a factor explaining the educational needs of children.[24]

The Plowden Report saw racial prejudice as playing little serious part in schools, but many people working with young children in urban areas during the 1960s and 1970s saw that the real needs of black children were not being addressed. These needs were not simply about a failure to assimilate, so people working with children set up mechanisms to support them by sharing cultures, such as learning to cook a variety of foods, using clothes from many cultures in the dressing-up corner and generally being friendly to each other. This is usually called multiculturalism (or multicultural education) and there was clearly nothing wrong with it in itself.

Lots of excellent resources for young children were produced. Some of them, however, while trying to address the needs of our multicultural society, gave inappropriate messages to children. For example,

one toy company produced a rag doll with a brown face, brown hands and brown feet. But the body underneath its clothes was white, with a join at the neck, wrists and ankles.

Some books and jigsaws reinforced stereotypes of black people, for example African-Caribbean men as bus conductors, Asian men as shopkeepers and African-Caribbean women as nurses. While these were positive images, they sometimes gave the impression that black people only ever did these jobs and were not likely to do something else.

Multiculturalism would have been ideal in a society where racism does not exist, but it could not even begin to address the underlying racist attitudes that many people held in Britain. The real problem was that it failed to touch the way that racism ranked cultures in a racial hierarchy, some being seen as more worthy, and therefore more powerful, than others.

Critically, multiculturalism failed to take account of what black people themselves wanted for their children. Furthermore, while it extended people's knowledge about other cultures it did not necessarily change their attitudes. For example, a racially prejudiced child might visit a home corner that represented a particular culture. The child would certainly acquire information during the visit, but without support and the opportunity to reflect on what they had experienced, they would be left with the potential to use that information as ammunition against the people of that culture rather than the chance to gain real knowledge of and respect for the culture and its people.

Multiculturalism was initially seen as only being applicable in multiracial areas. Largely white rural areas and city suburbs were ignored, except in places where a few people were seriously trying to deal with how children learn racist attitudes. It set up the concept that the 'issue' was about black people and where they live rather than about racism, which is nearly everywhere. It was not until the publication of the Swann Report in 1985 that this perception was, in some areas changed.[25] The Report drew attention to the need to address multiculturalism in all areas, mainly white as well as multiracial. What was needed, and is now becoming more widely recognised, was a clear strategy for addressing racism – an anti-racist strategy.

Lessons learned in the early years field

Since the mid 1970s there have been continual, constructive changes in the ways that prejudice and discrimination in the early years have been tackled

Learning from the past | **25**

in Britain. For example, there were extremely positive aspects of the 1989 Children Act and its accompanying guidance with regards to equality.[26] These demonstrate not only the effectiveness of people who worked long and hard for changes in the law, but a willingness on the part of national government to take changes on board in the legislation. This has resulted in much more serious attention being given by registration officers, inspectors who inspect under the requirements of the Children Act and people working with children to what equality means in practice.

At a more down-to-earth level it is now possible to buy dolls that represent boys and girls anatomically and which represent a range of skin colours realistically, although it has to be said that they seldom represent a range of accurate physical features and characteristics.

Changes in the way that racism and discrimination in the early years field are addressed have come about in many ways, for example through:

- laws;
- the development of specialist groups;
- national early years groups and organisations incorporating issues and concerns about racism in their training, organisation, publications and practice;
- the inclusion by national training and education bodies of discussion about racism in syllabuses and training materials;
- a vast increase in the availability of appropriate resources;
- black and anti-racist groups continually identifying and reinforcing what needs to be done;
- individuals thinking about and raising the issues; and
- networking on a large scale.

Over the decades, groups and individuals have campaigned for change by raising concerns and speaking at conferences, publishing articles and books, circulating relevant articles and videos, lobbying parliament, conducting research, organising conferences to discuss aspects of racism in early years services, meeting with key organisations and evaluating resources (toys, books, games and posters).

Since the change of government in 1997, there have been positive signs that issues of equality are to be addressed at a national level. As well as the requirement for Early Years Development and Childcare Partnerships to cover the equal opportunity strategy and ensure equality of access and opportunity in their plans, the Office for Standards in Education (Ofsted) has published nursery inspection guidance on equality of access and opportunity.[27] At time of writing, there are positive indications that the Qualifications and Curriculum Authority (QCA) will address equality issues in the revision of its document *Nursery education: desirable outcomes for children's learning – on entering compulsory education.*[28]

Furthermore, the Early Childhood Education Forum has fully integrated equality issues in its text, *Quality in diversity in early learning.*[29] This is a framework for practitioners to think about, understand, support and extend the learning of young children.

These changes by no means indicate that all is well or that all early years services and settings are implementing practice based on principles of equality. But they do mean that the issue of equality in the early years is firmly on the national agenda and that most national organisations are working towards equality at all levels. A fragmented approach is changing to a strategic one.

Tackling all forms of oppression is serious but not hopeless. It is important to recognise and acknowledge the positive changes that have occurred and to maintain a confident perspective towards the future – to remember the successes and not dwell on the failures. Working with allies: with men and women, with people of differing abilities and with black and white people is a constructive way to put our objectives into practice together. Most of the key issues that need to be addressed have already been identified – the rest is about supporting the necessary changes and making them happen.

5 | Thinking about racial equality

This chapter identifies some of the issues that arise when thinking about racial equality in early years services and settings.

Child-rearing practices

The idea that there is a 'best' way to bring up a child is rightly beginning to be questioned. You only need to look back over the past 30 or 40 years to see how attitudes and practices have changed with regards to white, middle-class babies to see how attitudes to child development and child-rearing practices can change among and between groups. For example, in the 1950s white British mothers were generally advised by professionals to feed their babies every four hours, regardless of whether they were hungry or not. Babies were often left to cry from hunger because the time was not yet up or forced to try and feed when they were not hungry. Later on, mothers were advised to feed their babies when they wanted it. These two opposing practices were advised by and within the same social group of people. Time clearly changed the idea of what was 'best'.

Bedtimes and sleeping

Bedtimes used to be strictly adhered to by most white middle-class families, not because the parents necessarily wanted some peace (although that might have been an extra motive), but because that was considered to be the 'best' thing for the child. Parents who didn't have their young children in bed by 7.00 were often regarded (by health experts, middle-class writers and other professionals) as inadequate or negligent. Few seemed to think that parents might enjoy their children's company or prefer not to limit their freedom. Black and working-class families suffered particularly from being wrongly seen as irresponsible in this matter.

Nowadays, notions of cultural superiority about child-rearing practices are less strongly held. Strict adherence to formal bedtimes is diminishing in white middle-class and other families, and most children go to bed later than they would have done 20 or 30 years ago. More people seem to believe

that, as long as children have enough sleep, it does not matter exactly what time they go to bed.

Ideas about where a child sleeps are also changing. Seeing and learning from what other people (other cultures) do has opened up discussion about the options available. Families, who 20 years ago would not have given a second thought to babies sleeping in any way other than the way they have always known now consider all sorts of possibilities. A baby might sleep:

- in the same bed as their mother;
- in a cot in their mother's room;
- alone in a separate room; or
- with siblings or other children in a separate room.

Most people now accept that there is no definitive right or wrong way to bring up a child and that it is possible to learn new ways of doing things from people with a different cultural background.

Meal times and eating

There are many different ways to eat food, all of which are appropriate to particular circumstances. Most children living in Britain will need to learn to use a knife and fork, but they should be able to do so in an atmosphere of equal and mutual respect for other ways of eating. In any case, not everything is eaten with a knife and fork. The whole basis of which implements are used at mealtimes is culturally and socially loaded. Toast, biscuits, fruit, crisps and peanuts, for example, are eaten with fingers. In British society, cake is eaten with fingers – except in certain posh situations when special little forks are provided.

Every family arranges its meals in many ways, together or separately, at fixed times or when they are hungry. Some sit round a table, some sit and eat their food on their knees and others squat or sit on the floor with or without a cloth on the floor. What might be the consequences if a child, who is eating happily at nursery, is met with a cry of: 'Don't eat with your fingers, it's rude (or dirty or unhygienic or uncivilised)? Other children who hear the phrase may be left with the message that people who eat with their fingers are rude, dirty,

Thinking about racial equality | **27**

unhygienic or uncivilised. The child herself may wonder whether her own family, who eat with their fingers at home, are rude, dirty, unhygienic or uncivilised. The likelihood is that she will become embarrassed about eating and reluctant to do so for fear of criticism or ridicule.

As long as children wash their hands properly before eating – a habit usually encouraged for all children before they eat – eating with cutlery, with chopsticks or with fingers should be equally acceptable. All require specific manipulative skills.

'Good manners'

The concept of what constitutes 'good manners' is probably well established in every society. It is so well established that whenever someone breaches the code of behaviour everyone 'in-the-know' recognises it immediately.

Good manners are learned. Children are programmed with them from a very early age – young children in white British society and in some other cultures are taught to say 'please' and 'thank you' almost from the day they are born. They are taught that it is open and honest to look someone in the eye when being reprimanded and that to look down is to be devious and to appear unrepentant. But children from many other cultures are taught that it is disrespectful to look someone in the eye when being reprimanded, so they cast their eyes down. There is a phrase in Grenada, 'Don't let your eyes cross me!' Children who meet someone's eye in this situation – as a white British child might do – may be seen as rude, disrespectful or ungrateful. Similarly, a black child who casts her eyes down in Britain may seem unrepentant.

Body language patterns of behaviour are deeply culturally loaded. When building up empathy and understanding, it is therefore important to learn about the differences in body language and not to take offence or misinterpret unfamiliar behaviour.

This does not mean that 'accepted' good manners should be ignored, but it does involve recognising and perhaps unlearning automatic negative responses to unaccustomed behaviour. A child who seems to be lacking good manners may simply have no knowledge or experience of learned patterns of behaviour – manners may be so routine among those in the know that they become meaningless. For example, when you say 'Hello, how are you?' do you *really* want to know how someone is, or is it just an automatic phrase?

If people do not take time to think about the way language is used there is a massive opportunity for misunderstanding and misinterpretation which may have serious consequences. Some languages do not have the words for 'please' and 'thank you'. Appreciation may be expressed in body language, built into the language or just accepted as being there without the need to say or do anything in particular. A white British person who has grown up here may be irritated by a Pakistani mother who says in English 'Get your coat' to her child, without adding 'please'. But the 'please' is implied in the changing inflections of tone, the body language and the facial features. There is no word for 'please' in Punjabi, and the Pakistani mother is speaking a language additional to her own.

Identity and self-esteem

Children's sense of personal identity comes from many aspects including their name, sex, skin colour, physical features, position within the family and language. Their cultural identity comes from their environment, who they interact with, the food they eat, the clothes they wear, the places they live in, the music they listen to and the spiritual values of their family.

When children attend an early years setting, other influences come into play. They learn who they are, where the rest of society places them in that society and what they feel about themselves. They learn if and how their language, culture, religion or skin colour are valued. This may influence how their identity develops.

The early years setting is in a crucial position to reinforce a child's existing level of self-esteem or to deny it. Where the setting understands and values all the aspects of a child's cultural identity, the child is more likely to feel comfortable and 'at home'. Where the cultural values are alien or 'strange', the child is more likely to withdraw into a protective cocoon or, alternatively, to lash out in anger. Where children's cultures are 'loved' they can more readily love themselves for who and what they are, and are more likely to be motivated to learn what the setting has to offer. The aim should be to integrate, as far as possible, the cultures of all children with the educational learning process.

Lots of positive support for all children – about who they are, how beautiful they are, how much their culture, faith, language and skin colour are valued – promotes positive identity. For white children there are many positive reinforcing images and messages around. But in a society where racism is endemic and so many negative messages about being black and about speaking a language other than English are received by black (and white) children, it is particularly important to

28 | Action for racial equality in the early years

give positive messages about being black and learning to be, or being, bilingual.

Black children's racial identity – their perception of themselves as belonging to a valued group – is important. Reflecting positive images and views about black children's identity is likely to have a positive influence on their future academic success. All children need to have positive identities and self-esteem to cope with fear, pain, confusion and the unavoidable aspects of life. This provides a stable core to their emotional health.

Everyone needs to feel good about who they are.

Naming

Your name is your face to the world.[30]

Most people are very particular that their names are spelt and pronounced correctly. Where young children from a variety of cultural backgrounds are involved this is just as important, but it takes time and commitment. Until recently, it has perhaps been assumed that where names are seen as 'difficult', shortened names or nicknames are acceptable.

But a name, like a language, is fundamental to a child's identity. If the name is unfamiliar, it requires effort to learn to pronounce it correctly, to understand the relationship between family and personal names and the order in which they are written or given. It may also require perseverance because some sounds are so unfamiliar to most English speakers that they find them difficult to pronounce. For example, with the Muslim name 'Tahir' (usually an Urdu word) the 'T' is pronounced as a sort of mixture between a 'Th' and a 'D'. It is therefore difficult to write phonetically and has to be repeatedly pronounced in order to learn the 'new' sound. Names often have religious or cultural connotations, so to pronounce them incorrectly may be particularly insensitive to devout families. And, clearly, it is wrong to talk about 'Christian names' in multifaith settings or where children do not belong to a particular faith at all. Instead, 'first', 'given' or 'personal' names may be more appropriate.

In recording a child's name the family name and first name should be identified as well as the sex of the child. Spelling names from the alphabet of another language may lead to discrepancies, with some names being recorded differently in the English script but being the same in their own alphabet. It is therefore critical to discuss with families what they wish their child to be called, how the name is pronounced, how it is written and in what order. It is also important to know the names of the family members because mothers and fathers may not share the same family name. The basis for understanding the naming systems is to learn about them from family members or from other sources.[31]

The concept of beauty

In most societies there is a culturally determined code of what is beautiful and many people, even within that culture, fall outside this definition of beauty. For white people, long blonde hair (and sometimes curly black hair), blue eyes and pink and white cheeks were once seen as the only recipe for perfection. The remnants of this are still around, for example in the large number of women who bleach or highlight their hair.

By these measures, there was no way that black people, particularly those of African origin, could ever really fit into the concept of what was beautiful, even if they wanted to. Many white people saw black people as incapable of being beautiful in the same way as white people could be beautiful, simply because of their skin colour and physical features. White people even ranked black people in a racial hierarchy of who they considered to be more or less beautiful. For example, women of Malaysian origin were often seen to be more beautiful than other black women.

To counteract this, the phrase 'Black is beautiful' was used in the United States during the 1960s to help both black and white people see that black skin colour and curly hair texture were also beautiful. The climate has changed somewhat since then. Despite claims by black models that the modelling industry subjects black models to racism, there are more black mainstream models than before, although most have relatively light brown skin colour (Naomi Campbell is a rare exception).

European fairy tales should be used only when great care has been taken to identify hidden (or not so hidden) messages of beauty. In 'Beauty and the Beast', the beast is nearly always black, while Rapunzel and Goldilocks are girls with stereotyped blonde hair, something that no black child can ever have. The stories do have a place in fairy tale history, and present mythical, if old fashioned, messages for Europeans. However, a range of role models are needed and examples of beauty and beastliness (where appropriate) should be seen in all skin colours.

Knowing about history and culture

We don't need to know anything about people from cultures different from our own in order to treat

Thinking about racial equality | **29**

people equally. But not knowing anything at all may look suspiciously like not being bothered to find out, which is hardly a basis for mutual respect.

Knowing about the history, culture and languages of people is nothing to do with not being racist. People can know all of this and still be profoundly racist and vice versa. But not wanting to know or not being curious about these factors does not bode well for helping all children to respect and value one another. Learning about differences is part of sharing together, and to learn about others should be an important aspect of satisfying one's own intellectual curiosity.

Knowing about a people's history in detail is less important than knowing about Britain's role in that people's history. Knowing something about slavery, colonialism and imperialism, about the origins of anti-Semitism and anti-Irish and anti-Traveller racism puts Britain's history into a context. It also explains how and why racism exists. It helps to explain how, in its various forms, racism started, how it was 'justified' and how, as a consequence, it became part of our society.

It is important to find historical and cultural information from authentic sources – from people themselves or, at second best, from reliable resources. Children's families are the best sources for what they do at home. But that doesn't mean that every family from that culture does the same thing. For example, some Indian families may eat fish and chips as often as English white people, and not every African-Caribbean family eats rice and peas. The best way to learn is to be part of a community, to genuinely want to learn and enjoy the different cultural aspects.

The problems in talking about racism

There are probably very few people who calmly accept being called racist. Only those who actively flaunt their racism are proud of the title and accept it as being the truth. They tend to flaunt it in large groups, and it is less certain they would be willing to admit to being racists when challenged as individuals.

Everyone else, whether they ever behave in a racist way or not, probably resists the idea of being called a racist. Why does this particular word cause such a reaction, often leading to outraged denial and upset? Is it a 'trigger' word? Cecil Gutsmore, a lecturer in Caribbean studies at the University of North London suggested at a seminar in London that there is a long list of words that describe aspects of racism, ranging from 'mild' words such as being 'patronising', through 'tokenism' to the very serious issues of 'legal discrimination', 'racial

attacks', 'slavery' and 'genocide'.[32] He suggested that when a white person is accused of one of these, perhaps of being patronising towards a black person, they react as if they are being accused of genocide. A trigger mechanism going up the list is set into action and the reaction is out of all proportion to the initial word used. Why is this?

Is it because, basically, most people don't want to be called racist because they know in their hearts that it is wrong? Basically they know that black and white people are all human. Is it because they know, whatever they may think themselves, that it is unacceptable to be racist in our society? They know that there is a certain generally agreed code of values that demands 'tolerance' towards all who live in Britain, whatever individuals may do. ('Tolerance' is a word frequently used to describe the way white people view black people. But the word itself is not positive – it means 'putting up with', not a phrase that describes positive valuing.) Even though some white people may make racist 'jokes', be unpleasant about black people or make 'unwittingly' negative comments, somehow they don't see this as racism. If challenged they will deny that they are being racist. They don't seem to make the connection.

The only explanation for this appears to be that even though these people may say or do racist things, they are ashamed to be *caught* at it.

The subject of racism, when raised among white people can be a total conversation killer. There may be several reasons for this inhibition. Perhaps the people in the group are afraid to talk about racism in case someone says they are a racist. Perhaps they don't like black people, but can't explain, reasonably, *why* they don't like them, so they clam up. Perhaps someone has had it pointed out to them, however sympathetically, that they have said or done something offensive in the past. For example, they may have called someone 'coloured' rather than black because they thought it was more polite. This can make people scared of doing the wrong thing and inhibited in their communication with black people.

Can black people in Britain be racist too?

Sometimes white people say that black people are racist too. If they mean that black people may be racially prejudiced, this is true. Black people may be prejudiced against white people or against people from other black groups than their own. There is no reason why, just because they are black, they cannot be racially prejudiced. But, in

Britain, what little evidence there is indicates that, despite their experiences of racism at the hands of white people, they are less racially prejudiced overall than white people.

Perhaps what is meant is that some black people are sometimes racially prejudiced against other black groups. This is also true. They may also imply that somehow this inter-black group prejudice justifies, or at least explains, the universality of racial prejudice and why white people may be prejudiced. If black people can be prejudiced then of course white people can be prejudiced too. In a sense they are perhaps saying: 'What's so wrong with it, then? It is natural, we can't do anything about it!' This is not true. There is some religious prejudice between some black groups and some black people are prejudiced against other black groups because of their histories and for other reasons. For example, some Asian people who left African countries under threat of their lives, are prejudiced against some African people and, in turn, some people from these African countries resented the economic position of Asian communities living there and so supported their evictions. But so far as can be assessed it is equally possible for both black and white people to be racially prejudiced.

The reality is that in some situations racial prejudice may manifest itself in personal racial discrimination. Hypothetically, just as a white woman might refuse to employ a black woman in her business because she is black so, too, a black man might refuse to employ a white man in his, because he is white. Both situations are possible and both could be unlawful under the Race Relations Act, according to the circumstances.

But, while there are some overt interracial conflicts, there appear to be a greater number of organised white groups who are explicit about their racial hatred against black people and who may, and do, use violence, than black groups who are explicit about their racial hatred of white people. Furthermore, some of the conflicts between black groups, allegedly based on religion, are more likely to be forms of local gang warfare.

However unpleasant, offensive and wrong they are, personal racial prejudice and discrimination are not the same as racism, although they are a part of the total package of racism. Racism in Britain includes the institutional and structural way that black people are discriminated against. White people do not experience these forms of racism in Britain. They are therefore in powerful positions with regards to black people, regardless of whether they want to be. Black people in Britain never have this form of power. While it would be possible for individual organisations run by black people to discriminate against white people, in the same way as happens in white-led organisations, they can never do this in the powerful, national, prestigious institutions and structures that dominate and control our society. No institution or structure should discriminate against anyone on racial grounds.

In Britain anyone may be racially prejudiced, both black and white people may be racially prejudiced. And both black and white people may practice racial discrimination in their personal behaviour. But only white people benefit from the institutional and structural racism endemic in our society. And only black people are subject to this institutional and structural racism. Because of these tensions, between some black and white groups, between some black and other black groups and between some white and other white groups (for example, in Northern Ireland) situations may arise where it appears that they cannot work together harmoniously or effectively. There are no easy solutions to such situations. The reasons for them are embedded in history. In all such situations there is a need for sensitivity.

Talking about racism in multiracial settings

Racism has often created difficulties when black and white people are working together to address issues of racial equality in the early years field. There may be no shared experience based on trust from which to work. In fact the differences in understanding and the different experiences of racism make it difficult for any group of people to work together in the field of racial equality. Even in all-white groups, people may need to learn to talk and listen to others before raising emotion-laden issues such as racism.

At some point, both black and white people may be able to recount the personal anguish they have gone through in trying to work in multiracial groups. This must be the height of a measure of success in terms of trust. To expose and relive those painful times and know that everyone accepts and understands what it was like is a considerable achievement.

Working in multiracial groups can be challenging. Some black and white people may never have sat down and talked with each other before. Both may come with fears and apprehensions, with anger and resentment. Everyone just has to try to understand this. It can be extremely painful and hurtful. Insensitive things may be said and once they are said it is difficult to unsay them. White and black

Thinking about racial equality | **31**

people are equally able or unable to express themselves endearingly.

It is vital to accept that this may be the very first time that a white person has appeared to want to listen to what a black person has to say and vice versa. Because of this, and because there is finally an opportunity to release the feelings of a lifetime, what is said may be difficult to hear, may be distressing and may appear to be out of all proportion. And black people as well as white people do not always get everything right. But taking time to listen to what people really feel is extremely important.

It may be helpful to forestall potential difficulties and differences of opinion by devising a way of communicating with each other beforehand – setting up some ground rules and a structure for discussion. And it may be helpful to meet somewhere that is neutral to everyone or to have an outside facilitator who is experienced in diffusing the situation if it gets out of hand.

There has to be a shared objective – the removal of racism in the early years. But it may be necessary to aim to achieve other objectives first. For example, to be able to talk with each other, then to decide what to do next – working with a series of objectives together before embarking on racism. Ultimately, the welfare and wellbeing of all children come first,

over and above any personal differences between adults. There is no miracle button to press. If everything appears to be going smoothly it may be necessary to think about whether people are suppressing their real feelings.

Sometimes early years groups may decide to split into white and black groups to work on particular issues or for particular reasons. Each may have something specific to raise. This may be one of the results of coming to terms with the legacy of racism.

Working in multiracial groups can be a tremendously exciting thing to do, a real learning experience, an opportunity to question and re-evaluate one's own experiences – but trust, respect and honesty are essential if multiracial groups are to work together against racism. Sharing ideas and exchanging information about such things as the range of cultures is not only interesting, it provides an opportunity to have long-held ways of doing things turned on their heads. For example, thinking about child development theories and the variety of child-rearing practices is one of the most enlightening, revealing and convincing ways to understand how easy it is to make negative assumptions based on cultural differences. To share ideas and practices across cultures is exciting, informative and, in a sense, liberating.

6 | Developing a policy for racial equality

A policy for racial equality should cover everything for which the Early Years Development and Childcare Partnership, the service and the setting are responsible. It is not just a statement of intention, it must be accompanied by an implementation programme and a monitoring mechanism to ensure the policy is being put into practice, otherwise it will merely be a paper exercise.

Policy development takes time, but it is time well spent if it is to be owned by all the stakeholders involved (families, children, people who work in the service and settings, representatives of the local community). It is really important to ensure that as many of the stakeholders as possible are familiar with the issues, understand their implications and are committed to implementing racial equality. Learning to talk together and trust one another are critical to developing an effective policy.

Several groups of people should be consulted in the run-up to developing policies for racial equality. Early Years Development and Childcare Partnerships should consult all stakeholders, for example families of young children from all ethnic groups and communities, including Travellers, refugees and asylum seekers. Early years services should consult staff across their service and share the results of the Partnership consultation with families. Early years settings should consult with all people working there, the families and potential families using the settings, children, governors, management and committee members, and relevant and appropriate members of the local community.

The consultation should include information about policies for racial equality (translated and interpreted where necessary), why they are essential, what they might mean in practice and how they are to be implemented and monitored.

A policy for racial equality should include the following.

- Policies on racial harassment (see Chapter 8).
- A statement of intent about racial equality in employment and all services for young children in the Partnership, the service and the setting. It should be specific about the areas of the service it is intended to cover. It should include everyone –

white, Jewish, Irish and black people, other minority ethnic groups, Travellers, refugees and asylum seekers.
- An implementation programme to address all the work carried out by the Partnership, service and settings, with timescales for how long it will take to achieve, who is to do it, any training and resource needs, including funding.
- A mechanism for regular monitoring of the policy's effectiveness and implementation programme. This will involve collecting and evaluating ethnic data on all relevant aspects of the Partnership, service and settings to identify any racial discrepancies. The monitoring is to look at groups, not individuals.[33] For example, in terms of children accessing the curriculum, it is critical to examine (usually by careful observation) whether any particular racial groups have less or more access to some of its aspects. Are bilingual children or children learning English as an additional language provided with the same learning opportunities as everyone else?
- Procedures for removing or rectifying any racial discrimination found, and a commitment to doing so.
- Careful analysis of all recruitment and admission arrangements to ensure that they are not racially discriminatory and that all job descriptions require employees to be committed to the implementation of racial equality in the early years.
- A method for keeping good records of children in the settings, including details of their full name, the name they are known by, date of birth, country of birth, religion, diet, ethnicity, first language, first language of parents or carers, any other languages spoken at home, any experiences of previous early years settings, health, and attendance at a supplementary mother-tongue class or school.
- A timetable for action on all the above.
- Clearly defined allocation of responsibility for implementation of policy at the highest employment levels and for action at every level.
- Regular reviews of all the policies, implementation programmes and monitoring mechanisms to check on their effectiveness.

Developing a policy for racial equality | **33**

Developing a policy without support

If there is no support for developing a policy for equality within the service, the only immediate way forward is by:

- persuasion through discussion with colleagues;
- encouraging others to read articles;
- developing a rationale for why a policy is needed, why it would be of benefit to the group and linking it to all inequalities;
- raising issues of concern at meetings; and
- asking for issues to be put on the agendas of management committee or governors' meetings.

Examples of what racial prejudice is and how it may be manifested in early years settings are often useful methods of helping others to understand what it actually means to children and their families. Real-life incidents from the service or setting are often more persuasive than theoretical analyses – and usually you have to touch people's hearts so that they realise the seriousness of what is being raised.

It may be hard to find allies and to reject accusations of being eccentric or as having a chip on your shoulder. However, it is crucial to do both of these. Link up with other people who are doing the same sort of thing and join national groups that work for equality. Having this kind of support helps to maintain a realistic perspective on the situation.

People are often fearful of setting up a policy for equality. They feel it may rock the boat and cause upset. They are afraid of what it might entail and they are afraid of the racism they might encounter. What they do not know or have the confidence to believe is that having a policy is actually likely to make life easier for them. A framework to refer to and an atmosphere of constant discussion reduces the fear of the unknown, and the process of policymaking helps prepare everyone involved to think about the issues through knowing and addressing the facts.

Building up the policy and implementation programme slowly but surely, and checking on how it is going all the time, are the fundamental principles on which to operate. Obviously, rushing in without careful thought and planning would be likely to give trouble. But, the policy can be seen as starting on the very first day that the first constructive discussions are held.

Early years settings and families

It is absolutely fundamental for addressing racial equality that the early years setting and families work together, as parents and other family members play a critical role in determining their children's racial attitudes. Children who experience a set of values about racism in the setting and a different set of values at home are confused. They may resolve it by avoiding it, they may make up their own minds and express what they feel, or they may keep quiet. The majority of families who visit the early years setting for the first time are usually happy to discuss the policy for racial equality in the context of looking at everything that is done. It is important to explain, at this early stage, exactly what it involves and to provide them with back-up written materials.

For families, the ability to see what goes on in the early years setting and to take part in its activities will demonstrate the value of being positive about differences. It is particularly useful if families work on tasks with settings, such as putting together the policy for equality development or the implementation programme. For example, families and those working with the children could, together, devise criteria for selecting resources.

Not all families have the same understanding of early years education and care. There are often distinct cultural differences and it is therefore important to give every family an opportunity to discuss ideas, share information and ask questions. This is particularly important where there is no common shared written means of communication or where some family members may be unable to read and write. Explaining what is being done and why, from the inside, will help families to understand, rather than feel that they are on the outside looking in.

Parents have many other commitments – work, caring for the rest of the family, personal lifestyles – that may influence their ability or willingness to contribute to the setting's activities. For example, more African-Caribbean mothers than most work full time, so they may find it particularly difficult to attend during the day.[34] Some families will be totally unfamiliar with the concept of participation so will not come until they feel comfortable. Others may be afraid of a possible 'Us and Them' culture, or be in awe of any form of educational provision. Some will attend regularly and others not at all. So long as everyone's needs have been addressed and all are equally welcome then all that can be done is to persist in trying to include everyone. One essential measure that helps to include black families is where black people are employed in the setting. For families where their children are learning English as an additional language, the employment of bilingual workers is particularly helpful.

Whatever happens and whoever attends, it must not be assumed that the people who attend ongoing discussions speak for the rest. Consultation must

34 | Action for racial equality in the early years

include all parents – none are representative of all others. This is critical when a black governor or member of the management committee is appointed. Although they are likely to have some experience of racism in common with other black people, they are no more likely to represent all black people's opinions and ideas than a white person would be to represent other white people. Unless there is some formal mechanism where an elected delegate is accountable to the electorate, full consultation should take place.

There has been a lot written recently about the importance of parental involvement and parental partnership.[35] The Children Act Guidance refers to the need to consult with and involve parents about the early years services in their area, including parents from all 'ethnic minority groups'. The recent Guidance on Early Years Development and Childcare Partnerships requires all Partnerships to ensure they have representation from parents, including parents in employment, and that the plans involve consultation to gain the views of parents and children 'in a range of languages for those who have English as an additional language'.[36] The principle of partnership with parents (and families) for the plans applies equally in early years settings. Care needs to be taken to ensure that all parents and family members are involved and that the involvement includes being equal partners in addressing racism.

To enter an early years setting where middle-class white values predominate must be daunting for those whose experiences are different. Creating an ethos where everyone feels 'at home' is very important though, once again, racism makes things difficult. What goes on outside the early years setting, in people's lives, comes into the setting as 'baggage'. Everyone has to learn to put up with it until they are confident enough to throw it away. Only then can real trust and equality be put into practice.

Families and children with 'mixed' cultural and racial backgrounds

Nearly all of us belong to 'mixed' backgrounds of one sort or another. But for some children the visible differences between their parents are more apparent than for others. Not everyone, white and black, accepts such families and their children. The children may feel confused about who they are and may have strong feelings about how they should be described. If one parent is black and the other is white they may learn, from society's values, that white is preferable. They may be referred to as 'black' because that is how society perceives them, but may not feel that they are black or wish to be

seen in any way to reject the heritage of their white parent. All these problems are the result of racism.

Melissa's mother is Indian and her father is white English. They live on a suburban new estate. Her family is very loving. At four years old, she started at the early years setting in the area and was immediately teased there about her colour. She didn't tell anyone at home about the teasing but she spent a lot of time at home washing her hands and body to 'try to get the colour off'. She didn't talk to her mother for six months.

When Melissa finally told her parents what was happening, they realised that they had wrongly thought that being a loving family would protect their daughter from feeling negative about her skin colour because of racism. Melissa had held her mother responsible for the pain she was experiencing.

It is important for children to be clear from the start about who they are and who their parents are. Lots of positive talk about skin colour differences, about cultural differences and an understanding of how positive self-identity and self-esteem develop, will help children to feel good about who they are. The difficulties that some children may encounter in building self-esteem are demonstrated by the lack of many good resources about mixed-race families, with illustrations and stories about them. Listening to parents and children sensitively about what they feel and how they wish to be described will help everyone feel valued and positive about who they are.

There are several specific issues that arise for and around families of mixed 'race' and parentage.

- If one of a child's parents is white, the family is often concerned that the early years setting will treat the child as white and make no attempt to address racism or provide a supportive environment.
- It is very important to maintain contact with the roots of both parents. This is not always easy if one family lives in another country or the parents no longer live together. It is critical to try and maintain contact with an extended family, even when no longer in contact with one parent.
- Parents have to deal with the racism their children may face. Unlike families where both of the parents are black, a white parent may have less experience, knowledge or even understanding of racism – let alone any idea of how to deal with it.
- White mothers in particular may have to face abuse and hostility from strangers. They are sometimes seen as 'slags' because they have

Developing a policy for racial equality | **35**

had, or are having, a sexual relationship with a black man. Their children witness this abuse. White childminders looking after black children sometimes also suffer from this – many have told of their experiences of racial abuse on the street. Others have given this as a reason for refusing to mind black children, seeing this abuse as categorising them as 'loose women'.

- Parents with children of a different skin colour than their own often have to face the surprise of others. The surprise suggests a suspicion that the children do not really belong to the parents and this can lead to disturbing incidents.

> Melanie – whose father is white and whose mother is black, and of mixed parentage herself – has fair skin and light-coloured hair. Soon after Melanie was born her mother began carrying Melanie's birth certificate around with her, as it was so often suggested that she was not Melanie's mother. These suggestions were sometimes threatening.

- Sometimes, children of mixed parentage or 'race' find that no child of any other racial group wants to play with them. Of course, this also happens to children who have two white parents or two black parents, but children of mixed parentage may feel particularly rejected because their parents may belong to the same racial groups as the children rejecting them.
- Some parents may have to face initial and possibly lasting racial hostility to their relationship from their own families.
- Parents may face questions like 'How black is the baby?', implying that to be 'too' black might raise difficulties of acceptance. Where children from mixed-'race' families have a range of different skin colours, the same questions about 'darkness' make everyone feel uncomfortable.

On a happier note, mixed-'race' families often report the positive changes they make to their own families. They often, for the first time, understand and try to address their own racism. They may all learn to be proud of their mixed extended family.[37]

Travellers and itinerant communities

The term 'Traveller' generally includes English and Welsh Gypsies (some of whom may be Romany), circus families, fairground families, Irish and Scottish Travellers (who sometimes call themselves Gypsies), Bargees, New Travellers and, more recently, European Roma. Only Gypsies have been defined in law as a racial group and are therefore covered by the Race Relations Act. The term Traveller is written with a capital 'T' to distinguish it from other travellers, for example, commercial travellers. The word 'Gypsy' is also written with a capital 'G' as they are recognised as an ethnic or racial group. The phrase 'Travelling communities' is used to describe people who are, or who have been, associated with a traditionally nomadic lifestyle. As with everyone, there is great variety in what Travelling people call themselves.

Travellers tend to experience more hostility than any other group. It is estimated that only about 20% of Traveller children ever attend any early years setting.[38] This is partly because of the hostility they face, partly because of their nomadic lifestyle, evictions from unauthorised land and lack of familiarity with educational settings, and partly because of their distance from and lack of transport to settings.

They are distinguished by their mobility and their connections with a travelling way of life. Those who are not living in houses are highly mobile and the number of moves that individual families make has increased since the repeal of the Caravans Sites Act 1968. This removed the requirement for local authorities to provide sites for Travellers and so left fewer authorised sites. The Criminal Justice and Public Order Act 1994 has exacerbated the situation, as police and local authorities now evict people more quickly from unauthorised sites. This has led to an increase in the number of Traveller families who are in emergency housing, often against their wishes.

The number of actively mobile Travellers has not decreased mainly because of the lack of authorised sites. Families who live in houses may still travel in the summer. This mobility has many implications for early years settings, not least the day that children are 'counted', which may mean that a place for a Traveller child, who is absent on the counting day, is not funded.

For children of statutory school age, there is funding from the Government to support local authorities in their work with Traveller children and the Traveller education services. From April 1999, there is also specific funding for pre-school Traveller children.

In order to overcome hostility in early years settings, it is important to have a policy of respecting all children and being explicit about including Travellers. A policy involving discussions with families prepares the way for everyone to be equally accepted. Refusing to accept Gypsy children to an early years setting because they are Gypsies would be unlawful.

36 | Action for racial equality in the early years

It is more likely that Traveller children will be accepted into a setting if an Early Years Development and Childcare Partnership supports its equal opportunity strategy by referring to the particular needs of Traveller children in its plan. Furthermore, if the plan requires all children to be accepted in a setting where there is a place available then, if Traveller or any other children are refused places because of who they are, the Partnership could decide to take action against the setting.

The only way of assuring that all children are equally welcome is to give parents, children and people working with them the opportunity to discuss, consider and support a policy that gives equal access. If children and their families come to understand that everyone has a responsibility to welcome one another, prejudice against Travellers may be reduced. However, there is no easy solution to such prejudice and perseverance is needed.

Working with families who disagree with the setting's policy for racial equality

While co-operation between families and settings is one of the surest ways to implement a successful anti-racist policy, people working with children must address racism even where families are unsupportive or hostile. Racism is wrong and must be worked against whatever the circumstances.

Where a parent or other family member does not agree with the setting's policy for racial equality, further discussion may need to take place on another occasion. There are principles about the policy which are not negotiable, for example the fundamental *principle* of opposing racism is fixed, while the *methods* for countering it need to be flexible and open to new ideas.

A serious dilemma arises if, after some time, a parent refuses to accept the fundamental principle.

- Should the parent's child be accepted into the setting to give them an opportunity to hear ideas that they may not hear at home?
- Or might the child's presence (and that of the family members) make it difficult and uncomfortable to be positive about equality?
- More seriously, might the child or a family member say or do something that is hurtful to or about black or other minority ethnic children and their families, whether they are present or not?

A decision about whether or not to accept the child into the setting will have to be made according to the circumstances. It is important to bear in mind

always that people do change their minds, that they do sometimes admit that they were wrong. If this happens it is not a time for gloating but for rejoicing that changes are always possible.

The situation is less serious if the principle is accepted but the methods are challenged. Such disagreements may encourage the setting to positively consider the methods they use from another point of view.

If a family objects to a policy after seeming to have accepted it at first, further discussion is needed. For example, a mother might say that she does not want her son to play with dolls (let alone black dolls), or she might comment that there are too many black children in the setting. There is no easy way to deal with situations like this, but openly accusing this mother of being racist will not achieve anything. The most important thing is to persuade her to reconsider, perhaps by reading something, [39] talking to someone else (perhaps another parent or a governor/manager) or coming into the early years setting to see and understand what is going on in practice. It is important, however, to state at an early stage that the policy of the setting is clear – that it values all children equally.

Working in these situations requires skills, patience and determination to overcome any apparent barrier – and it may take a long time to succeed. All those working with children need to practise dealing with a variety of complex situations.[40]

Working in mainly white areas

Due to the absence of many black or minority ethnic people in mainly white areas, there are some very specific considerations to bear in mind when working with families. [41]

1 *Avoid patronising or even romanticising black or minority ethnic people. Avoid the temptation to focus on the exotic by concentrating only on festivals and special cultural practices or taking a 'them' and 'us' approach*
All work needs to be carefully planned and prepared, in consultation with parents, children and those working with them. This means analysing and understanding the real reasons for wanting to acknowledge our multicultural society in as natural way as possible, perhaps by thinking and comparing how white people might wish their culture to be introduced to people from other cultures. This may take time.
2 *Prevent the setting from being labelled as 'loony left' or as having a 'bee in its bonnet', otherwise anti-racist ideas may be dismissed at the start. Get allies before you start*

Developing a policy for racial equality | **37**

Go in gently but with a firm understanding of why it is important to establish and implement an anti-racist policy. Be armed with lots of examples of what the policy might mean in practice.

If there is already a policy for equality, it should provide the starting point. Everyone is to be equally valued, so every aspect of life in the setting has to be examined to ensure that is happening. This is the beginning of the process. It might be appropriate to start by looking at the resources and then going on to consider the number of languages spoken by or cultural backgrounds of the setting's children and their families. This establishes a profile of the variety of people in the setting, which can then be extended to a wider area and the whole of British society.

If there is no policy or framework within which to work, it is crucial to form alliances with other groups trying to work in the same way. If there is no other such group locally, then it is essential to contact local or national organisations for support. There is a list of useful organisations on pages 66–67.

3 *Address the fact that all role models, visitors, parents or people working with children are white*
In multiracial areas, the reality of diverse cultures is ever present and so there is nothing artificial about helping children to value the racial, cultural and other differences between people. This may not be so easy in largely white communities, although there are always some differences between people that can act as a starting point. For example, there will be different family structures (one parent, two parents, step-parents disabled parents, families with adopted or fostered children), probably different languages and certainly different accents. Once the principle of valuing difference in general has been introduced, work to help children value racial and cultural differences should be easier.

Resources reflecting our multicultural society cannot replace the presence of people from different 'races' and cultures, but they can still be very effective. For example, a variety of cooking utensils in the home corner help to represent diversity between people and their different ways of living.

4 *Find a solution to the lack of appropriate resources and of real financial support*
The way that resources are used is critical. Even where there is a total lack of resources reflecting our multicultural society and where there is no money to buy them, it can still be possible to raise issues of valuing the differences between people. While it is easier to talk about skin colour differences if you have dolls with a range of skin colours, even white people have different coloured skins, hair and eyes. That could be the way into talking about other people – using photographs and posters. Used as part of the curriculum, these conversations can provide many starting points to discussions with young children.

5 *Raising the principle of a policy*
Sometimes, with an ally, the issue of diversity can be raised in terms of gender, sexual orientation, disability and racial differences. Talking about getting a policy for equality might be a way in for some people to give their support.

6 *Getting started*
If managers are not interested in establishing a policy but the staff of a service or setting are committed to doing it, they can always get together, train themselves on the issues involved and then, armed with knowledge, begin to put pressure on their managers to make it happen. For example, one member of staff in an education department started to think about the issues and, with a few others, organised and ran initial and in-service training courses. Later, two other interested members of staff joined the authority and, together, they set up and funded a group of about 10 trainers from all the relevant sectors – statutory, voluntary and private – with the specific purpose of addressing equality issues. This group organised training sessions for themselves and then trained their particular groups in turn, thus acting as a cascade mechanism. They also organised conferences and ran training courses for early years settings where they were asked to do so. Although the whole process of change took more than 10 years, it has proved very effective. The group itself has now been going for eight years.

To make this kind of set up possible, an understanding of and commitment to equality issues should be a key factor in the Early Years Development and Childcare Plan, and in the job descriptions and person specifications of senior staff. Access to some form of funding is critical if regular meetings, hiring speakers and training days are to be possible at low cost to participants.

Creating a no-blame culture

One of the difficulties of addressing racism in early years services is that white people with basically good intentions, but who display racist thoughtlessness, will be appalled by the suggestion that they are racist or that their actions could be seen as racist. Whether the 'accuser' is black or white makes no difference. In these situations, people are often overcome by being 'charged' with

38 | Action for racial equality in the early years

racism. They may become defensive and vehemently deny that anyone could consider their actions or language to be racist. Their mortification then prevents them from reflecting on the issue.

An equally complex problem is that black people may sometimes respond negatively to being reprimanded, criticised or chastised by a white person in the course of a working day ('You're only saying that because I'm black'). They may respond in this way without thinking, without distinguishing between whether the white person is behaving in a racist way or is simply making a work-related comment. The power of racism to cause these situations has to be recognised and addressed.

Whatever the truth of the situation, emotions have got in the way. Somehow, the emotional heat has to be dampened so that objective thought can be brought into play.

Responding to emotions – a case study

One early years setting tried to address emotional reactions to racist issues by creating a 'no-blame' culture with the parents, their children and those who work with them. It started with the officer in charge recognising that issues of racism were difficult to discuss without people getting uptight and defensive. Such emotional responses prevented everyone from arriving at satisfactory solutions to the problems that were being discussed. After a series of meetings, the officer suggested that they all try to think about discussions around racism solely in the light of professionalism, in relation to the work they were doing. This no-blame culture had three fundamental principles:

- no one was to react negatively to criticism from any source;
- no one was to blame anyone or feel righteously superior; and
- there was to be absolute acceptance that everyone makes mistakes, everyone can learn from them, and that learning only happens when people do not feel under threat or threaten someone else.

This last point is a distinct parallel with the way that children learn – they cannot learn effectively if they are fearful or insecure.

After some adjustment and time, everyone in the setting supported the approach and began to work together using the three no-blame principles. For example, a black key worker felt a white mother was avoiding her, even though the worker had a particular responsibility for her child. She felt the white workers encouraged this by taking over her

role with the mother. Instead of complaining about it to the officer in charge, as she might have done in the past, the black worker felt able to talk openly with the white workers concerned. She started by trying to look at the situation from the mother's point of view, by asking the other workers to consider the following questions:

- Was she (the black key worker) doing something that might be affecting the mother's relationship with her?
- Was she as welcoming as she might be?
- What was the mother's perception of the worker's relationship with the child?

All the workers then looked at the situation from their own point of view.

- How did the black key worker perceive the behaviour of the white workers?
- How did they perceive her?

Having considered these issues together in a supportive environment, they were able to make suggestions as to the way forward. The white workers accepted the vulnerability of the black worker as a result of her experiences of racism elsewhere. They also accepted that they may not have sufficiently encouraged the mother to talk with her key worker (the black worker). This was due to their efforts to be helpful to the mother, rather than to any negative view of the black worker. The black worker accepted their genuine wish not to take over her role and that, because of past experiences, she had misinterpreted their actions. To clarify matters, everyone agreed to properly follow the setting's policy for parents to discuss their children with their key worker whenever possible.

Of course, the black worker's analysis that the white workers were colluding in racism could have been correct. If that had been the case, the setting's staff would have had to face the issue in the same co-operative spirit.

Another positive effect of the no-blame policy was seen when a little Asian girl said to one of the white workers, 'You don't like us, do you!' After some discussion with the girl, the worker discovered that, at story time, she never asked 'them' questions about the story she was telling. The worker thought about it and realised two apparently unconnected things:

- most of the Asian children in the setting sat at the edge of the story-telling group;
- she only ever involved the children sitting near her in discussions about a story.

By thinking objectively about the day-to-day reality of the children's behaviour and of her own practice,

Developing a policy for racial equality | **39**

the worker was able to 'see' the situation from the Asian girl's perspective. To her, it had appeared that the worker didn't like Asians. In a racist society where even a little girl may have experienced racial hostility from white people, it is understandable that she had interpreted the worker's actions in this way. The worker understood this and, without being defensive, she was able to change her practice and try to vary the places where the children sat and how they asked questions.

What came out of the whole no-blame process was a development of trust, empathy, co-operation and happiness in this early years setting. The whole ethos changed it into a place where people listened to each other without taking offence, where constructive comments were given and received positively, where respect and understanding became the natural order of the day and where children, those working with them and families all clearly benefited.

For those wishing to establish a no-blame culture, it is a good idea to suggest that people work within existing teams or existing relationships. The principle behind the culture can also be fostered with children, for instance during circle time (see page 42).

Establishing a multiracial workforce

There are more black people working in the early years field than 10 years ago, although they still do not reflect the percentage of black people in the community. In one survey, there were more people from an African-Caribbean background working in the early years than from an Asian background.[42] However, fewer black people of any racial group worked in the higher status, higher paid areas of the service than white people.

Whatever the reasons for this – and some at least are due to racial discrimination in the education or employment system – to be a truly multiracial workforce, black and white people need to be employed roughly in proportion to their numbers in the community, and at all levels. Apart from the justice of this, black people need to be seen as role models and as successful as white people by all families and children alike.

In mainly white areas, a multiracial workforce is unlikely to be achieved. But in other areas, realistic targets for achieving such a workforce should be set. While it is unlawful, under the Race Relations Act, to set quotas (giving favourable treatment to a fixed number or percentage of the workforce) for employing people from particular racial groups, it is not unlawful to set targets to ensure that the aim of increasing the number of minority ethnic employees is kept on the agenda. This does not mean giving favourable treatment to any ethnic group, as no recruitment practices and procedures can favour any group on racial grounds. (For a full explanation of how this policy can work, see the section on the Race Relations Act, page 47–50.)

Positive action can be taken to increase the number of black and minority ethnic employees when there are very few or none already in the workforce. (See section on positive action, page 49.)

Before considering positive action to create a multiracial workforce, it is crucial that the service or setting demonstrates that it is committed to such a workforce by adopting as many aspects as possible of the framework for implementing policies of racial equality (see Chapter 9). A setting that already puts racial equality into practice is far more likely to attract black and minority ethnic applicants to work there than one that does not do so. Advertising posts in places likely to be seen by black and minority ethnic people, going out and meeting and talking to them, using local community languages to spread the word and passing handbills around are all things that could be considered.

After doing all these things no one should be discouraged if changes to the workforce do not occur immediately. Building up a reputation for being welcoming to all, for valuing the presence of black and minority ethnic children and adults in the setting and for being genuinely committed takes time. It may be a fact that no person wants to be the first black or minority ethnic employee, as the risk of an unhappy experience may be too great to take. This is all part of the process of change.

Talking to (and consulting with) black and minority ethnic families may reveal circumstances that explain the lack of applications. Every avenue should be pursued. At the end of the day, the fact that the setting has tried hard, is a place where everyone is equally valued and respected may have to suffice for the time being. Keeping open minds and ensuring effective training is in place for all employees and volunteers should continue.

Once a workforce is multiracial it should be a matter of priority to make sure that everyone has equal access to in-service training and support. Career progression should be open to everyone on equal terms. It is not enough to be satisfied with a multiracial workforce if all decisions are made by white people. Even if this is so, there are ways of involving everyone in discussions, valuing everyone's contributions and eliciting ideas and suggestions that reflect people's cultural experiences. This can be done informally or

40 | Action for racial equality in the early years

formally, by having regular agenda items to consider equality issues at meetings and ensuring that people are able to raise concerns in an atmosphere of trust.

Meeting together in racially specific groups

Sometimes black (or white) people working in early years services or settings may wish to meet separately from the others to discuss specific issues of concern to them. This may cause some friction – other people feeling that they are being talked about and that the others are being given preferential treatment. If everyone sees that discussions are exclusive for a positive purpose this should cause no anxiety. For example, black people may wish to meet separately to talk about being black in a largely white workforce. However, in general, such meetings should be about empowering the participants as part of a short-term strategy with a concrete programme of action. Such a meeting would be very unlikely to take place during work hours and certainly not if the staff from other racial groups were not able to have an equivalent time for meeting if they so wished.

Working with young children

Play resources

There is now a wealth of resources that reflect our multicultural society, although cost may influence what early years services and settings can actually buy. These resources cannot create a positive view of society by themselves; changes will not come about just by the presence of resources that reflect our multicultural society – it is the way that they are used and the way adults and children involve them in their play and curricular activities that are the critical factors of change.

- If a new black doll is left in the box and ignored, the children may receive subtle messages that the doll is not 'wanted'. Instead of the doll helping to create a positive view of society, these messages may reinforce negative messages about who is valued in society.
- If dual-language story books are the only multicultural resources in a white monolingual playgroup and nothing active is done with them, they cannot help children understand the reality of our multicultural, multilingual society.

The key to ensuring that everyone is valued equally is to think carefully about what the children might already have learned about people who are different from themselves. Those working with children have to know why the issues are important, should be able to answer questions from children or their families and anticipate what the questions might be.

It is important to grasp the fact that even if families have migrated to live in Britain from somewhere else, they are here now, so it is life in Britain today that is relevant to the children, rather than the lifestyles of people in, for example, Asia, Africa or the Caribbean. This is not to ignore the heritage of children whose families have migrated here, it simply puts that heritage in context. Consequently, pictures of families from a variety of cultures who are living in Britain and doing ordinary everyday things in Britain are the real reflections of a multicultural society for children.

The existence of a properly implemented policy for racial equality will have prepared everyone – those working with children, families, the children and others – for such circumstances. They will have thought and talked about how to use the black doll and the dual-language books effectively. Those working with children will have thought about how they might respond to any questions that the children might ask. In this situation a child's reaction is more likely to be one of curiosity rather than rejection, for example 'Why is the doll black?' or 'Why do black people have pink palms and soles to their feet?' The way adults use the resources is important in setting an example to children.

Involving families in organising workshops or discussions about resources is particularly important as they are likely to acquire books and toys for their children at home. Those working with children and families can, together, devise checklists or guidelines for selecting them. Thinking about the criteria to be included helps everyone to understand why they are important.

Ensure that a *range* of resources is available:

- a range of skin colours and physical features in book illustrations and posters;
- know the correct names for cooking pots, musical instruments and clothes used for dressing up and how to use them and
- when planning pre-numeracy and science or technology activities, include materials that reflect the lives of a variety of people.

Ensure that the resources reflecting our multicultural society are used actively, in positive ways, and not just left lying around. The way that resources are used by adults and children are critical for giving strong messages that they are a full part of 'normal', everyday learning activities.

Provide accurate images of people living around the world, living in Britain and in the local community.

Developing a policy for racial equality | **41**

Talk about people from all racial backgrounds who have contributed to the local and general culture, literature, sport, inventions and history in a way that young children can appreciate and understand. Provide photographs of people from various parts of the world as well as in Britain depicting their lifestyles, houses, food, work, dress and leisure activities. Be careful to select those that represent life now, using accurate terminology to describe things and to counter 'typical' stereotypes.

Dolls are particularly important in children's play because they are the nearest representatives of real people, although it is almost impossible to get accurate representations of anyone. White children have plenty of role models of white people around them, so the accuracy or otherwise of dolls is perhaps less important than for black children, who have fewer positive role models. It is therefore essential that great care is taken to avoid stereotyped or 'golliwog-like' dolls that may reinforce negative imagery for all children. Dolls' clothes should reflect a variety of cultures.

Dressing up clothes should also represent a range of cultures, for everyday and special occasions. Some should be kept separate because they represent particular special occasions and should be treated accordingly. Where miniature clothes are collected, they should be from all cultures and not just representing those of people from minority ethnic groups, for example, not just small-sized *shalwar kameez*. Names of clothes and how and when they are worn should be known. Ordinary clothes in different colours can also be useful, for instance to illustrate that in the Hindu culture brides wear red, while white is worn at funerals.

There are several guidelines and checklists setting out criteria to use in selecting and evaluating resources that promote equality.[43]

Books, pictures and language

Looking at books and illustrations, and being read to, all play an important part in children's language development. They also provide opportunities to learn about scripts, their variety and the skills needed to write them. Some are written from left to right, some from right to left and others from top to bottom, some rest on an imaginary line while others hang from it. The variety is yet another measure of the variety of people. Children and adults do not have to be able to understand the detail of the text in order to appreciate the script. Dual-language books help children to respect and admire scripts that are different from their own. When there is someone present who is able to read the second-language text alongside the English words, the diversity of language can be heard in practice.

Encourage all children to speak their home languages as well as learning English as an additional language. Seek advice and guidance about how best to help children to learn English. Where necessary, try to get expert support for the children's language development. Obviously, bilingual and multilingual adults have much to offer but everyone working with the children should reinforce the value of linguistic diversity in personal ways. Introducing languages, dialects, accents and scripts (including sign language and lip reading) that are less familiar and knowing how they are written, read and understood is a way of breaking down language hierarchies.

In these ways children are helped to recognise the skills needed and the advantages to be had from learning, singing, rhyming and speaking languages other than their own. There are many dual-language story books available.

Circle time

Circle time provides an opportunity for open discussion about any joys or conflicts that may have happened during the day, and for questions or issues to be raised in a way that is appropriate to the children's ages. The discussions can be models for children to learn that differences can be positive, joys can be shared, conflicts resolved peacefully, talking about something can be empowering and that everyone has something to learn. Discussions may focus on something that has happened outside the early years setting, something that children have witnessed or seen on the television, or a local carnival.

Some rules need to be agreed for circle time, for example, rules about not interrupting, and accepting comments, feelings and ideas with respect. Circles can be big or small depending on the circumstances. Children are usually able to express what they think if they feel confident and free to contribute their thoughts in a supportive atmosphere.

Persona dolls

Another way of addressing specific issues is to use persona dolls. They are special dolls that do not live in the toy basket and who can represent particular 'people' or be characters in a story. For example, one doll could be a Gypsy child. Where he lives, what he does, what he might think about can be made part of a story. Other children can then talk

42 | Action for racial equality in the early years

about what they might have in common with him – perhaps they live in or have had a holiday in a caravan or trailer.

Persona dolls can be used to introduce children to differences that do not exist in the setting, to extend their awareness of diversity and to counter racism in society. They are particularly useful in developing children's concepts of understanding what is just and fair, and of learning to be critically aware of the world around them. They are important in introducing and developing children's negotiating skills to talk about things together and how to work together and help each other. The stories can be planned or spontaneous.

Notions of empathy can be discovered and built on. If and when a child from a different racial background comes to the setting (in the case of the example above, a Gypsy child), children will already have thought about him and what he might be feeling. Is he apprehensive? What could they do to help him feel at home? They can take the doll home and tell their families the story about him as well. They can make up their own stories about a doll.

Persona dolls can also be used to address an issue of concern, perhaps one that has arisen during the day, either in or out of the setting. For example, if there has been some name-calling, a story could be told about what this means – for the name-caller or the person called. Again it helps to focus children's mind and thoughts on a person, at one step removed, so it is not threatening but may cause a child to think and reassess attitudes. This method backs up the sort of work that is done in circle time. [44]

Celebrating and responding to festivals

If an early years setting wishes to celebrate or respond to the various cultural and religious festivals in our society, the people working there need to ask some searching questions about their current and future practice.

- Do we celebrate all the festivals or do we only celebrate Pancake Day, Bonfire Night, Easter and Christmas? Do we really know and understand what these celebrations celebrate?
- Do we try to think about less familiar festivals?
- Do we celebrate only those where children in the setting practise them at home?
- How do we celebrate them if there are no children or families from that culture or religion to help us?
- Is there a difference between 'culture' and 'religion' in this sense, because everyone has a culture but not everyone has a religion or faith?
- How can we 'celebrate' with reverence and respect a religion that we do not practise, or more seriously, one that we might profoundly disagree with?
- How do we avoid paying only lip-service to cultures and religions?
- How do we ensure that we value each culture and religion equally – especially when most of the children in the setting are from a majority culture and religion?
- Does celebrating festivals reinforce the 'exotic' aspects of different cultures rather than the ordinary everyday experiences? For example, are Christmas, Easter, Diwali, Eid-ul-Fitr, Rosh Hashana, Hanukkah and Guru Nanak's birthday so embedded in the particular cultures that they represent critically important aspects that each culture stands for?
- Do we celebrate festivals in the desire to 'share' the cultures and religions that make up our society?
- Are they shared equally and with equal respect?
- Why do we celebrate various cultural festivals in the early years setting anyway?
- Are there, in reality, more everyday, ordinary, common-or-garden things that we can do to learn about each other?
- What, if anything, does knowing about 'other people's' festivals do to help us to counter racism?

These are complicated interlocking questions that may baffle us. People will have different answers to the questions. Even so, there are fundamental principles that should be behind our practice in this area.

- People from all cultures and faiths should be equally valued and respected.
- Everyday and ongoing valuing and respect for difference is more important than what we do on special occasions.
- We need to involve all families in what we do, while bearing in mind the principles and commitment to racial equality.
- Acknowledging, respecting and celebrating a religion is not the same as believing, practising or participating in it.
- We cannot celebrate a particular festival and then do nothing about the people whose festival it is for the rest of the year.

If parents object to celebrating particular festivals, it is usually the result of lack of communication between workers and parents.

Any festival that is celebrated must be as authentic as possible. In multicultural, multifaith areas the

Developing a policy for racial equality | **43**

resources for accurate implementation of the celebration are present or readily accessible. Where this is difficult, for example in a largely white or specific suburban area, are there other ways that children can learn about, and value, people from different cultures? On the other hand, if they only celebrate their 'own' festivals how will they learn that other people (those not living in their area) also have festivals that they celebrate? And, in any case, there are only rarely areas where everyone is white – most areas have at least one or two restaurants run by Asian or Chinese families. Even so, these families cannot be assumed to be willing or able to be 'used' as examples of our multicultural society.

In such areas it is essential to prepare for the celebration by visiting the teachers' centre or other resource centres, getting accurate and appropriate resources, and talking to relevant people. Accepting that the celebration may not be perfectly implemented is part of trying to get it right. Evaluating the resources used, after the events, is critical in operating open-mindedness and thinking how the celebration might be better conducted next time.

Celebrating differences

We sometimes hear people working with young children say that they 'treat all the children the same'. On reflection this is unlikely to be true. We rarely treat any child in the same way as another, because they are all different from each other and require and deserve treatment to reflect these differences. Parents of more than one child will realise that, in practice, they do not treat their children in exactly the same way – they deal with them in the most appropriate way according to each child's personality, capabilities and needs. What they do usually *do* is to treat them all *equally.* That means that they receive equal access to things that are important, but not necessarily in the same way.

When people say they treat children the same, they probably mean that they think they are equally important and wish to give them equal chances. If children are treated in the same way, it is likely that some children will not have their needs and differences acknowledged. Treating all children as if they were white and middle class would not be giving all an equal chance. Providing food that is familiar to most children but unfamiliar to some is treating them all the same, but the effect is that some may find it easier to manage than others.

There is a need to think about differences very carefully so that 'different' is not seen as 'bad' or 'wrong'. Professor Steve Jones made this point in his 1991 BBC Reith lectures:

People look different. Difference usually means classification; and it is only a tiny step from classifying people to judging them.[45]

We can value differences and similarities by talking about them, by discussing our different skin colours, hair textures, eye, lip and nose shapes, temperaments and abilities, as well as our common humanity, our concern for others, our need to eat and sleep and our need to be loved. We can also learn to respect other forms of difference, for example the different places where we live, the type of homes we have, whether we have lots of money, sufficient money or do not have enough money to live on, whether we are quick at learning things or not so quick, whether some of us who are not so quick have other skills and attributes that we can value, whether we are extrovert or introvert, whether we dress like everyone else or differently. Most of these issues are culturally loaded. Some value judgements, such as whether someone is 'beautiful' or 'plain' are particularly culturally subjective and require great sensitivity when discussed.

All children are children. All children (and adults) should treat others and be treated fairly. Children enjoy playing games, they (nearly always) have a home, but they have a variety of family structures and family members. They all wear clothes but they are different for different occasions. Most of them see films and videos at home, but they may be very different. This range of similarities and differences is more obvious in multicultural areas, but in largely white areas children also have a range of similarities and differences, and they can form the basis for talking about differences and similarities in society at large.

It is important not to pretend there are no differences. Of course, we are all human beings but we are all different from one another. It is a good thing that there are differences between us, so long as our differences do not mean anyone is of less value. When differences are not acknowledged it is often because those differences are not valued equally with the cultural norm. It is easier to ignore differences altogether than to draw attention to the fact that they are not equally respected.

Differences between us extend our knowledge of the world, they put us all in perspective and enhance our lives – so long as we let it happen.

Religion

The difference between religions raises very different issues from those raised by different languages, cultures and racial groups. It is quite clear that each of the latter should be accorded equal value and treatment. While this should also be the case with religions, the situation is much more complex.

While some people respect the right of others to practise their religion, and believe that there are many ways to express a faith, others profoundly disagree with this. They believe that their religion is the only true one and that believers of other religions are wrong, or even sinners. This opinion might be part of the doctrine of their own religion.

In trying to address the complex problems surrounding religious differences, early years services and settings need to consider the following principles.[46]

- Children of any religion or no religion should be treated with equal concern.
- All religions should be respected, though people from some religions may not be able to say that they have 'equal respect' for others.
- Religious practices, requirements and needs should, as far as possible, be accepted. However, this should not mean that in the workplace, some people do less work than others, contribute less or have fewer responsibilities, as a result of their faith. This would be unfair to those of no faith or those whose 'traditional' celebrations come during early years setting holidays.

  Where particular religious requirements clash with the setting practice, this should be resolved, wherever possible, through negotiation. For example, a religious Jewish worker in a setting that stays open until 6.00 in the evening may not be able to work after 3.00 on a Friday during the winter (Jews may not work on the Sabbath which runs from sundown on Friday to sundown on Saturday). In this case, a shift pattern with other workers may be helpful. Where it is not possible to negotiate a perfect solution, other less acceptable solutions may need to be agreed. This should not, however, override the principle of equality of treatment for everyone.

  The issue of religious holidays is particularly difficult for the workplace. Unless everyone's religious holidays are given as days off for all workers, there will be inevitable problems to face as some people may end up having more days off than others. It is impossible to decide which religious holidays 'deserve' to be taken as days off and which do not. To alter the long-established Christian holiday seasons (Christmas and Easter) could have serious consequences as it may cause

a setting to be closed for a holiday when the adults who use it have to be at work and therefore need to leave their children in the setting.

- No child should be discriminated against because of their family's religion. If discrimination on grounds of membership of a particular religion disproportionately affects a particular national or racial group, this may be unlawful under the Race Relations Act.
- Where an early years setting refuses to accept the requirements of the Children Act, to have regard to religious persuasions other than their own, registration and inspection officers will need to consider the specific circumstances of the setting. Discussion over time may lead to an acknowledgement of other faiths and some level of acceptance. It may be necessary for the group to have a particular form of registration.
- If possible, special diets for religious reasons should be made available in the setting. If it is not possible, families should be encouraged to supply their own prepared food. Where food is prepared on the premises, care must be taken about using separate cooking implements. Food that is unacceptable to a particular group on religious grounds must be kept separate from other food. It is better to provide vegetarian food (which is acceptable to all groups other than vegans) than be unable to offer a range of diets for children, at least on some occasions.
- Except in groups whose basis is on religious grounds, specific religious practices should not be observed. Certainly, no child should ever be required to practise a faith that is not their own.
- Families and staff should discuss any religious needs or requirements.
- Where adults and children are unable to take part in certain activities because of their faiths, this should be accepted and, where necessary, explained to the others.

Trying to make religious issues as unproblematic as possible is important if the principles of implementing racial equality are to be achieved. The Race Relations Act 1976 and the Children Act 1989 have laid down certain parameters with regard to racial discrimination and registration for early years settings. If matters cannot be resolved satisfactorily, it may be appropriate for some form of legal resolution to be sought in order to clarify the situation. However, registration forms should not concentrate solely on religion to the exclusion of other aspects of promoting a policy for racial equality.

Developing a policy for racial equality | **45**

7 | The law on racial equality

Over the past 20 years or so there has been considerable change with regard to racism in the early years field. The issue of racism is now on the national agenda, and this is a considerable achievement in itself. Even so, racism still exists in the early years, and some white people working with young children are reluctant to take positive steps against it.

Many white people living in rural, suburban or even multiracial areas refuse to accept that racism is an issue for them. This is not necessarily because they hold racially prejudiced views or because they are unconcerned about racism when they see or hear about it in the media. It is usually because they:

- have not thought about racism being relevant in their area;
- do not recognise the situation for the black people living in the area;
- do not recognise their own position of privilege by being white;
- do not understand the need for early years services and settings to consider what needs to be done about racism; and
- do not recognise that young white children may be part of the mechanism that keeps racism going.

Raising the issues in such areas requires enormous commitment, sensitivity and understanding – it is an incredibly important task to be undertaken.

However much racism is on the national agenda, the fact that many people fail to recognise it as an issue for them means that much of the organisational procedures and practices remain untouched. While the majority of early years services and settings pay some lip-service to the reality of our multicultural society, there are only a few who understand the reality of how racism works, know what needs to be done to counter it and are able to put it into practice. There remain many nurseries, playgroups, pre-schools, crèches and childminders who have not yet addressed racism seriously, and a few where ignorance or hostility prevail.

Guidance, consultation documents and reviews

1 The 1999–2000 planning guidance on Early Years Development and Childcare Partnerships has a section on equal opportunities which states that the Partnership

needs to ensure that the Plan promotes equality of access and opportunity for all children to be cared for, to learn and make progress whatever their sex, age, attainment, ethnicity, special educational need, disability or competence in English.[47]

It requires all services to 'offer equal opportunities to children and appropriate places for families from different cultural, ethnic and religious backgrounds'. In addition, the planning guidance requires Partnerships to show how they intend to cover the needs of all children from all communities.

Using relevant data about the area, they should consider which groups of children face significant obstacles in accessing or deriving benefit from early years services and for what reasons, including children of refugees and from specific religious and cultural communities. The Partnerships must show how they will reach these communities, for example through local forums and Traveller Education Services. Outline details of the policy for the education of children with English as an additional language should be given.

This is the first time that the early years sector has ever had equality issues so firmly on the agenda. Now, the DfEE approval of Early Excellence Centres requires them to have an equal opportunity strategy. However, although the DfEE highlights EYTARN's publication *Planning for excellence*[48] in the planning guidance, drawing attention to the framework for equality that is contained in it, the DfEE itself needs to define what the phrases on equality issues in the guidance mean in practice, what are the components of a strategy and how Partnerships and the DfEE can ensure their implementation through plans and Early Excellence Centres.

2 The 1998 consultation paper on the regulation of Early Education and Day Care, published by the DfEE and the Department of Health, asks questions about how to 'secure equal opportunities for all children' and what 'standards should be set to ensure that equal opportunities are provided for all children'. This is a positive opportunity to influence the content of the Regulations with regard to ensuring racial equality.

3 More consultation documents were published in 1998 – including the National Childcare Strategy (DfEE) and the draft framework for qualifications in the early years sector.[49] At time of going to press, the review of desirable outcomes for children's learning (QCA) was being circulated for consultation.

4 In 1998 Ofsted published guidance on equality of access to nursery education.[50] This is the first time that such guidance has been made available to nursery inspectors. Although it is very short, it makes some useful points about issues of racial equality.

Major legislation

Two pieces of legislation strongly influenced the way that early years services dealt with racial equality:

• Race Relations Act 1976; and
• Children Act 1989.

Together, these laws provide a framework for Partnerships, elected members, officers, policymakers, lawyers, administrators, trainers and providers to plan and operate a service which is based on principles of racial equality. In a sense the Race Relations Act is the 'stick' to ensure that discrimination is removed while the Children Act is the 'carrot' to ensure that what goes on in those parts of the service and settings for which it has responsibility treats all children with equal concern. They need to be considered together, each backing the other up. For example, any provider in breach of the Race Relations Act should be refused registration under the Children Act.

The two laws provide the rationale and the principles on which the Early Years Development and Childcare Plans can deliver 'the equal opportunity strategy', required by the DfEE planning guidance.[51] For example, while the Race Relations Act requires ethnic data to prove discrimination, the Children Act guidance refers to the need to collect such data.[52]

Race Relations Act 1976

Laws against discrimination cannot change people's attitudes, but they can change people's behaviour.

The Race Relations Act defines the forms of racial discrimination that are unlawful. It does not cover every form of racism but is specific about types of discrimination and the circumstances in which they might occur. Only people belonging to a racial

group, as defined under the Act, are covered by the legislation.

In the Act, a racial group is a one that is defined by reference to 'race', colour, nationality, citizenship or ethnic or national origins (Jews, Sikhs and Gypsies are covered, among others). Discrimination on racial grounds means discrimination on the grounds of 'race', colour, nationality, citizenship or ethnic or national origins. Note that the grounds do not include religion, culture or language, all of which are explicit in the Children Act 1989.

The Act identifies four forms of discrimination:

1 *Direct discrimination* This means treating a person less favourably – on racial grounds – than another person is, or would be, treated in the same or similar circumstances. For example, it would be unlawful to turn a child down for a place in an early years setting simply because they are black or white. The reason or motive behind the treatment is irrelevant. This form of discrimination is usually based on personal prejudice.

2 *Indirect discrimination* This means applying a requirement or condition which, although applied equally to everyone (all racial groups), results in a considerably smaller proportion of people from a particular racial group being able to comply. In cases of indirect discrimination, that racial group will be disadvantaged by their inability to comply and the requirement or condition itself will not be justified on non-racial grounds. This is similar to the form of institutional discrimination described above on page 8.

   An example of indirect and unlawful discrimination might include giving preference to applicants for an early years setting who live in a particular catchment area if this unjustifiably excludes an area where people from a particular racial group or groups live. Another example might be the insistence that girls wear skirts, which may disproportionately affect Muslim girls who are required by their faith to cover their legs. (While Muslims are not covered under the Race Relations Act as a 'racial group', they may largely be from a particular geographical area or nation that is covered. The skirt rule may therefore be indirectly discriminatory and unlawful.)

   Customs, practices and procedures which may have been in place for a long time, and were never intended to discriminate, may nevertheless have an indirectly discriminatory impact on particular racial groups.

   This form of discrimination is important because it reveals examples of practices and procedures where there was never a motive to discriminate but which, in practice, have that effect.

The law on racial equality | **47**

3 *Victimisation* A person is seen as being victimised if they are treated less favourably than others in the same circumstances because it is suspected or known that they have brought proceedings under the Race Relations Act or given evidence or information concerning such proceedings, or alleged that discrimination has occurred. For example, refusing a child a place at an early years setting *because* their parents had previously complained about racial discrimination in the setting would be unlawful.

4 *Segregation* Segregating a person from others on racial grounds alone, constitutes less favourable treatment. For example, grouping children at mealtimes or for play activities according to their racial group, and for no other reason, would be unlawful.

There are other sections of the Act that are also relevant to early years services and settings. They include:

- discriminatory practices
- instructions and pressure to discriminate
- aiding unlawful acts
- advertisements
- associations
- charities.

For example, regarding pressure to discriminate, it would be unlawful for the person in charge of an early years setting to put pressure on a college not to send them a student on placement who is of a different racial group from the children. The reason for the pressure is irrelevant.

Specific areas where discrimination may occur are defined in sections covering employment, education, services (including early years organisation and settings not covered by education) and vocational training. A duty is placed on local authorities to eliminate racial discrimination and to promote equality of opportunity between persons of different racial groups.

Monitoring commitment to the Race Relations Act

Coming to terms with the details and implications of the Act is not easy. Action should never be taken without a real knowledge and understanding of the legislation. Further detailed information is available in the Commission for Racial Equality's publication *From cradle to school.*[53] Advice is also available from the Commission and local racial equality councils.

To ensure that a commitment to racial equality is being put into practice, information should routinely be collected on the ethnic origins of people in the early years service and settings. Data on job applicants should be collected, with information about selection processes, job offers, promotion, access to career opportunities and training. Ethnic data should be collected on applicants for places in early years settings, selection processes and offers of places in the settings. This data should be analysed to check whether any racial groups appear to be less successful than others. Any discrepancies found do not necessarily mean that unlawful racial discrimination has taken place, but they do mean that the reason(s) for such discrepancies should be examined.[54]

Members of local black and minority ethnic communities should be consulted about collecting ethnic data regarding the terminology to be used, bearing in mind the reasons for collecting it and any need to compare data nationally. Extreme care must be taken in explaining why the data is being collected, how it will be collected and stored, who will have access to it, what it will be used for and what will be done about it if any discrimination is revealed.

Collecting and analysing data will only reveal patterns of differences between people from different racial groups, it will not show whether a particular individual is being discriminated against. This can only be done by comparing their particular circumstances with someone of a different ethnic or racial group. This may be done by seeking information from that other person, the person(s) alleged to have discriminated and/or taking out a complaint, under the Race Relations Act, in an industrial tribunal or in a county or sheriff court.

Exemptions from the Act

There are a few ways that the Act permits discrimination on racial grounds. These are strictly limited and specifically defined. They are intended to moderate the consequences of past discrimination and disadvantage, to encourage and make known to applicants that they are welcome to apply for jobs or training, or to address certain situations where being of a particular racial group is important. They include:

- employers and other persons encouraging people from under-represented racial groups to apply for work or training;
- recruiting a person from a particular racial group where being of that group is a 'genuine occupational qualification'; and
- taking action to meet the special needs of a particular racial group in regard to their education, training or welfare, or any ancillary benefits, according to the particular circumstances and other actions.

Although these forms of action are lawful it is never lawful to favour any particular racial group in the actual recruitment and selection process for employment.

In early years services and settings the exemptions listed in the three bullet points on page 48 might be used in the following circumstances, and are addressed in the sections of the Act shown in the headings.

Taking positive action[55]

Training for particular work – Section 37

When the Race Relations Act was passed it was only possible for an officially recognised training body to be covered by this section of the Act. Now any person or group may offer training under this section.

Any person may provide members of a particular racial group with access to training for particular work or encourage them to take advantage of it so long as people of that racial group have been under-represented in that work at any time within the previous 12 months. For example, if there were very few people of Bangladeshi origin either working in playgroups or trained in playgroup work in the area and someone or some group wanted to offer training in playgroup work specifically for Bangladeshi people, that would be lawful. It would also be lawful to offer transport and childcare specifically for this group of people.

This might be a way of ensuring that Bangladeshi and other children were looked after by Bangladeshi people as well as people from other racial groups, where this was appropriate.

Encouraging applicants into employment or training – Section 38

If an employer wants to have a multiracial workforce that is representative of the ethnic composition of the local community, or wants to convince (or try to convince) potential employees that applicants from the racial group in question are really welcome, then the employer can lawfully advertise this fact. The advertisement can state that applicants for training or work are particularly welcome from that racial group, but only if that group has already been under-represented in the workforce at any time in the previous 12 months.

The exemption only provides a level playing field with regard to applying for jobs or training, so that under-represented groups are specifically mentioned and encouraged but they do not get favourable treatment at job selection.

Special needs – Section 35

This section permits action to give people of a particular racial group access to facilities or services to meet their special needs in regard to their education, training, welfare or any ancillary benefits.

Special needs, under this section of the Act, are not the same as special educational needs in education law. Special needs under the Race Relations Act are usually defined as being needs 'that are either different in kind from, or are the same as but particularly greater than those of the rest of the population'.[57] For example, an early years project could be organised specifically for refugee children to address their recent experiences and to help them come to terms with their new lives in Britain.

Care needs to be taken in using this section of the Act to ensure that the needs really are 'special'.

Other exemptions

These exemptions are not about taking positive action, but address specific situations.

A genuine occupational qualification – Section 5(2)(d)

If an early years setting has a significant number of children from a particular racial group and few or no people working with the children of that racial group, it might be seen as important or helpful to the children to employ someone of the same racial group to support their particular needs. For example, it may be a good idea to employ someone who speaks the same language as the children. An advertisement for such a post can state that someone who speaks that language is required, and it would not be a breach of the Act to do this because the condition is not on racial grounds (anyone of any racial group is able to learn and speak any language).

The desire to employ someone of a particular racial group on those grounds alone must be considered under Section 5(2)(d) of the Act in order not to be discriminating unlawfully.

Being of a particular racial group is defined as a 'genuine occupational qualification' for a job only where 'the holder of the job provides persons of that racial group with personal services promoting their welfare, and those services can most effectively be provided by a person of that racial group'. In other words only a person of that racial group is able to perform the job effectively. If there are no existing members of staff of that racial group who are capable of carrying out the required duties and who it would be reasonable to

The law on racial equality | **49**

expect to perform these duties, then it may be possible to seek to employ someone under this section of the Act.

For example, if all (or nearly all) of the people working with the children in an early years setting are white and a large percentage of the children are of African-Caribbean origin, the organisation may wish to employ an African-Caribbean worker to support the children in a way that only an African-Caribbean person is able to do effectively. Young black children – who are growing up in a society where they experience some forms of racism – may feel more comfortable with a person who seems familiar to them, particularly when they are upset. That sense of familiarity may only be provided by someone of the same racial group who understands their culture, home life, dialect or language and family relationships. Employment of such a person could therefore be seen as conducive to the children's welfare.

This in no way suggests that white adults in this kind of early years setting would not be kind and supportive to a black child. Instead, there is a sort of parallel with the way that young children will run to their parents even when other familiar and kindly adults are around. However, the fact that racism exists has to be taken into account when understanding how a black child might perceive a situation and might react. In distress, they are more likely to seek comfort from a black adult than a white one, however supportive the white ones are.

It is not possible to determine, in advance, whether such an exemption would be possible under the law – only a court could decide that. So it is critically important to assemble all the facts, together with the relevant arguments about why only a person of a specific racial group could do a job effectively, before advertising the post under Section 5(2)(d) of the Race Relations Act. Legal advice should be sought first, from the Commission or from a racial equality council.[56]

Employing nannies – Section 4(3)

It is lawful, when recruiting someone to work in a private household, for example, as a nanny or an au pair, to select someone on racial grounds. Under the Act, working in a private home is not the same as working in the world outside the home.

Membership of associations – Section 26

An organisation of more than 25 members that has a constitution which regulates admission to membership, is allowed to restrict admission to a particular racial group, so long as it does not refer to colour.

For example, a synagogue, Irish, Pakistani or Jamaican group could set up an early years setting only for the children of its members. It could lawfully refuse admission to children whose parents were not members of the organisation.[58]

The weaknesses of the Race Relations Act

The Race Relations Act is a limited tool for addressing racism.

- It is difficult to prove discrimination and get evidence that compares the experiences of people from other racial groups.
- Tribunal chairs and county and sheriff court judges do not always understand racial discrimination cases.
- Cases take a long time to pursue and they are stressful. Legal advice, support and advocacy are now being made more available, but it can be a lonely business in taking up cases of complaint. Legal aid is not available in tribunal cases, so more funding and support are needed.
- Ultimately, the Act is about what you can't do, what is unlawful. It has nothing to say about what you *must* do in order to remove racism.

There have been only a few changes to the Act since it was introduced, and its failings have been pointed out to the government by the Commission for Racial Equality, as it is required by law to do.

If more people understood the Act better they would realise its creative potential. They would know that comparative data is an essential part of proving discrimination and that a threat of using the law can be a powerful tool for complainants to use against respondents in getting equal treatment. In some ways, the Act is in its infancy and its potential is untested.

The Children Act 1989

For the first time in the history of childcare legislation, the Children Act refers to the need for local authorities to give 'due consideration to the child's religious persuasion, racial origin, cultural and linguistic background' when making decisions about children in their care. When considering whether the daycare they provide is 'seriously inadequate', local authorities are required to 'have regard' to these factors in terms of the needs of the child and whether to cancel registration. The Act also requires local authorities to 'have regard to the different racial groups to which children within their area who are in need belong', when making arrangements for the provision of daycare.

The guidance accompanying the Act states that local authorities should:

50 | Action for racial equality in the early years

- 'provide a range of services which should reflect (in scale as well as type) the needs of children and families from ethnic minority groups';
- take account of cultural and linguistic needs;
- ensure that ethnic minority groups are consulted about policy and practice and that resources and food are appropriate to the children's cultural and religious backgrounds;
- recognise and respect the different backgrounds of the children, value them and foster their sense of identity;
- provide a service that values a child as an individual without racial stereotyping;
- have equal opportunity policies, including arrangements for monitoring and reviewing progress towards implementation and data on the ethnic origins of the local population, to ensure that the educational and care services are operating in a non-discriminatory way.

With regard to the registration of daycare, the guidance suggests that local authorities consider the following points when determining whether a person is 'fit' (that is suitable) to 'look after children aged under eight'. The person should have:

- 'knowledge of and attitude to multicultural issues and people of different racial origins';
- 'commitment and knowledge to treat all children with equal concern'.

The weaknesses of the Children Act
The Act requires local authorities to consider if daycare is seriously inadequate with regard to a child's religious persuasion, racial origin, cultural background and linguistic background, and whether registration should be cancelled. It should have similar requirements for the registration of daycare providers in order to prevent later situations occurring where cancellation has to be considered.

The law on racial equality | **51**

8 | Challenging racism and harassment

Racist instances in early years practice tend to be along the following lines:

- Child to child, eg white child to black (Indian) child: 'My mummy says that 'Pakis' stink!'
- Child to adult, eg white child to black key worker: 'I don't want you to touch me.'
- Adult to child, eg white adult to black child: 'Speak English, not that gobbledigook!'
- Adult to adult, eg white parent to white parent: 'There are more and more of those Asian kids taking over our nursery. It'll soon be like Pakistan here.'

Racial harassment, on the other hand, may be hidden under apparently acceptable behaviour. It is therefore important not to accept everything at face value – not to assume that all is well when it might be quite the opposite. All of those working with young children should keep a particularly watchful eye on how they behave together. Sometimes it is only careful vigilance that identifies what is really going on in an apparently 'happy' play situation.

Most days Shenaz tried to be near Jennifer, the member of staff who supervised children's outside play in the setting. Jennifer always welcomed Shenaz, who appeared a little shy and nervous. At the same time she encouraged Shenaz to play with a group of girls who she seemed to have played happily with on several occasions.

One day, Jennifer took Shenaz over to the group, who appeared to welcome her. Jennifer then moved away and returned unobserved, only to discover that the apparently 'happy' play involved Shenaz being teased and pushed about. The girls were calling her a 'Paki' and saying that she ate 'dirty rubbish food'. The behaviour was quite different from what it appeared to be from the other side of the play area.

On other occasions early years workers may be so involved with their own immediate situation that they fail to link it with what may be going on outside the setting.

An early years setting on the outskirts of a town had three black children. Two of them were siblings in a Nigerian family. The staff were becoming increasingly concerned that they were not 'settling in' and that some of the white children were ridiculing them because of their appearance and because they spoke Igbo together. They asked an adviser to visit. As she walked along the building next to the setting she noticed racist graffiti, written large, on the walls. When she mentioned it to the people working with the children, none of them had seen it even though they all walked by it every day. The Nigerian children's parents also walked by it every day.

Might there have been any links between the graffiti and the situation of the Nigerian children in the nursery?

While it is clearly the responsibility of everyone to address racism, it is specifically the responsibility of white people to deal with it. Whether they wish for it or not, white people benefit from racism and need to understand the often invisible power they hold. Sharing this power may mean giving up some previously held privileges. White people also need to take particular care to address the issue of some white children's often unconscious arrogance about who they are and their identity. This might be done by providing them with experiences demonstrating that black children, or adults, can do some things better than them (not because they are black but just that they have a personal skill) and that this is not a problem for anyone – that skin colour has nothing to do with it.

Immediate responses to racist incidents

Some 'racial' incidents may be the result of thoughtlessness. The lack of thought is, in itself, 'racist thoughtlessness' rather than an overt intention to be racist. Any incident where an adult, for example, tells an Asian child that she is 'not eating properly' when she is using her fingers or describes an African child's hair as 'kinky', needs to be dealt with immediately to maintain the child's

52 | Action for racial equality in the early years

self-esteem. In these cases, the child would need immediate support in the form of a positive endorsement of the value of eating with fingers or a happy, open discussion of all the different types of hair that the world's people have. Circle time can be used for this (see page 42).

However, this sort of incident also requires an approach that will enable the adult to really understand their own thoughtlessness and to make positive changes. Countering or challenging racist instances between adults is difficult because the person challenged will be unlikely to welcome it. They are likely to feel threatened, embarrassed and defensive. Should the event be ignored? Should it be dealt with at a later date? And was it really racist or are things being read into what is innocent? There are no easy answers. A public dressing-down for being racist is unlikely to help, as no one responds well to being humiliated. If an adult is made to feel bad in this way, their self-esteem and their ability to think clearly will drop. This will prevent them from being more thoughtful, rather than help them towards it. If the same person is presented with the issue in private and without being 'blamed', they are more likely to remain confident and be willing to look at the concern raised in an objective manner. This is particularly important where people have had negative past experiences of some forms of 'racism awareness training'.

Ideally there should be an ethos where people can say things to each other in a mutually supportive way. Creating an atmosphere where issues can be addressed openly, in a no-blame atmosphere, is discussed on pages 38–40.

Countering racist attitudes (where there are clear notions of racial superiority) from young children is very different from dealing with the racist attitudes of adults. We know that children have not yet had the opportunity to consider other information and points of view so we address the situation particularly sensitively. On the other hand, when there is a clear racist intent, it is necessary to be specific in condemning the action. The aim to bear in mind, after supporting the victimised person (child or adult), is 'What is the most likely way of addressing this situation so that the person concerned will listen, understand, consider and change the behaviour?'

Many racist instances are accidentally overheard. They are not addressed specifically to the person who overhears them or are said, 'nudge, nudge, wink, wink', between colluding white people, who would not have said or done what happened if a black person had been present. People who overhear such things have to judge how best to deal

with the incident, and whether to leave it until later or respond to it immediately.

The principle is that such an incident cannot be ignored, especially when it involves the early years setting itself, except in specific circumstances. For example, according to the circumstances, someone who overhears a racist comment might counter with one of the following statements:

- I'm sorry you think that.
- I don't agree with you.
- What makes you think that?
- What makes you say that?
- That's not my experience.
- Please do not include me in that.

Procedures to counter and prevent racist instances

There are clear procedures to countering racism in a situation where there is a perpetrator and a victim. The incident may be verbal or physical.

After identifying an incident as racist – whatever its level of severity – the first priority is to comfort and support the child or adult who has been victimised. The following steps should then be taken.

1 Make sure that anyone listening to or overhearing the incident understands that what was said or done was wrong, hurtful and unacceptable.
2 Support the child or adult who has said or done something racist while, at the same time, making sure that they know it is wrong, hurtful and unacceptable, and that it will not be condoned. Explain why. Take care not to undermine the child or adult's self-esteem by ensuring that the incident itself, and not the child or adult, is dealt with. Try to tap into their concepts of empathy to what it feels like to experience racism and, where appropriate, consider raising this sort of issue in circle time.
3 Where appropriate, talk about the incident with the perpetrator and the victim.
4 Follow up the incident with whatever strategy is necessary to prevent it happening again, according to the circumstances and the incident itself. Work with children, staff and parents, as appropriate.

People who tell a racist 'joke' sometimes don't see it as racist. The very least to be done in these instances is to register objections, quietly and with authority, and if possible, give the reasons why in as light-hearted a manner as possible, so the teller is able to go away and think about it without feeling defensive. This is far easier if one is confident, has experienced this sort of thing before and is

Challenging racism and harassment | **53**

committed to doing something about it. It is important to try to get someone to think about what they have said, rather than humiliating them in public (especially when he or she has been so up front about the 'joke'). It is best done in a non-threatening way and, preferably, on a one-to-one basis. If the 'joke' is overtly and intentionally racist it is, in some ways, easier to deal with by being explicit about your disagreement. The teller knows it is racist even if they don't care.

It is vitally important to provide black and other minority ethnic children, who may experience racial harassment, name-calling or bullying, with the skills to deal with them. Such children have few positive or useful alternatives in reacting to these forms of racism, and there are three common negative responses.

- Children might ignore them and pretend they have not happened, bottling up the pain inside themselves – and some time in the future this is likely to burst out in anger.
- They might respond by calling names back. But there is no racist abuse against white children and adults that comes anywhere near the offensiveness that black and minority ethnic children might experience. Calling someone 'Honky', 'Whitey' or 'Chalkface' are mild terms compared with 'Wog', 'Coon' or 'Paki'. These latter words are loaded with historical and offensive implications. In any case the argument may be that to return words in kind is to stoop to the level of the perpetrator.
- They might lash out physically, and are then likely to be blamed for being violent.

The common experience for racially abused children is to be reprimanded or punished for retaliating, with little recognition or understanding of what harm it does them or of the cumulative effect of such situations. The only real alternative for them is to tell someone what is happening. All children and adults need to be part of a system that has policies, procedures, responsibilities and monitoring systems in place to counter racial harassment and bullying in general. An adult or child can only safely 'tell' in a service or setting where others will take responsibility and do something constructive about it, where they will be comforted and their pain acknowledged, and where they will not subsequently be victimised. It is no good a child reporting something if an adult says 'Oh, dear, let's just try to forget it' or 'Just ignore it', or if the adult tries to divert the issue by making distracting suggestions such as suggesting everyone does a jigsaw together.

Children can learn to take responsibility to tell adults when they witness any form of unkindness,

racial abuse or name-calling. Young children can be encouraged to recognise it happening to themselves and others and to tell an adult, without going through the feeling of believing that they have betrayed a member of the group. If they can be helped to see that both the victim and the perpetrator will be supported, they may be more willing to come forward.

Children also need guidance about how to respond when there are no support mechanisms. Children could make use of all the following forms of self-defence:

- strong self-esteem;
- clear understanding that the 'problem' is with the racist abuser, not with black and minority ethnic children;
- forms of repartee.

All three forms of self-defence are built most strongly if families and individuals work together to provide the children with the tools of their defence and the confidence they need to use them.

Name-calling

All forms of name-calling are totally unacceptable, however innocent they might seem. Name-calling picks a child out, usually because they are different in some way. Children have often suffered this kind of abuse in silence, not even daring to tell their families what they were going through. This protective silence, the dread of telling on the others, has often prevented adults from realising the full extent and pain that some children experience.

While name-calling is always unacceptable and always wrong, it has particular implications for black children. Personally insulting names like 'Four Eyes', 'Big Ears' or 'Dumbo' are cruel. But when a black child is ridiculed for being black, the child's family and whole racial community is also being made fun of. It is therefore important to recognise the particular anguish that a black child may go through, while at the same time dealing with every incident of name-calling in a similar manner.

Having a policy on harassment

It is extremely important for a policy on harassment to be included in the policy on equality. Everyone working with children, all children and their families should know about it, understand what it is for and, wherever possible, have ownership of it themselves (never assume that a child who harasses another has parents who don't care; they may strongly support the setting's policy and be unaware of what their child is doing).

54 | Action for racial equality in the early years

Consistently raise issues of valuing and respecting everyone. Deal with every incident as part of the procedures identified in the policy.[59]

Very young children may not always interpret a racist incident as such, but older witnesses will be able to recognise whether it is racist. A racial incident is one where the victim (if they are not a very young child) feels or believes that what happened was because of their racial background. Every such incident should be taken seriously and not pushed aside with a casual reproving comment. Consider how seemingly innocent comments may be hurtful. For example, describing someone's hair as 'fuzzy' or someone's skin as a 'nice light colour'. Subtleties and innuendoes play havoc with how people receive such comments when racism is around.

Record all incidents and monitor them on a regular basis to check whether any patterns emerge and whether any particular children are harassing others or being harassed, and whether particular issues need to be addressed. Identify any future work that needs to be done with children or parents and families to ensure that what has happened does not recur.

After a racist incident, take the opportunity to talk with children, to explain that what happened was wrong and emphasise that what a person does, not who they are, is what matters. Talk with parents about what their children are doing or being subjected to, and seek their support in dealing with it in an organised way.

Challenging racism and harassment | **55**

9 | Planning for equality across the early years service

Keep in mind always the present you are constructing. It should be the future you want.[60]

Countering racism in the early years is a process, not a one-off activity. It must be strategic, planned for and effective. An ad hoc approach, where some aspects of early years services and settings are addressed for racial equality but others are not, results in failure to dismantle racism overall, ignores the interlinking mechanisms that continually reinforce it and leads to frustration for those who want to implement anti-racist practice but appear to be working in an unreceptive environment. Unless an anti-racist policy is planned and organised, different family work conditions, ability to pay, availability and access to early years settings will also combine to make it impossible to consider racial equality objectively.

The Government's 1997 decision to define a structural way of organising early years services by integrating all aspects of the service has made it possible to get away from operating ad hoc methods of implementing racial equality and to develop a strategic approach. Local authorities are required to form a Partnership, and the Partnership must devise an Early Years Development and Childcare Plan to include the equal opportunity strategy. The Partnership must also ensure that the plan promotes equality of access and opportunity for all children to learn and make progress whatever their age, sex, level of attainment, ethnicity, special educational need, disability and competence in English. This means that the responsibility for implementing racial equality can at last be defined – it lies firmly with the Partnership.[61]

Each early years sector (including the Partnership) needs to be examined as a whole and every aspect analysed, including employment, across all early years services and settings and all the practices and procedures that make up its organisation. Evaluating the sector in this way will make it possible to examine:

- whether discrimination exists;
- how it operates;
- what solutions are most likely to remove it; and
- what resources and training might be needed.

This strategic approach means that there is a real chance of effecting change, of removing racism and of implementing racial equality in early years services and settings.

Areas of responsibility within the local early years sector need to be identified and this can be done through analysis of all work undertaken by or covered in the Partnership, service and settings, plus their organisation, procedures and practices. For example, the Partnership is responsible for everything that is in the Early Years Development and Childcare Plan. The service is responsible for the employment of staff, training, administration and ensuring the implementation and monitoring of the setting policies. The setting is usually responsible for employment, involvement of any volunteers, the arrangements for admissions, the curriculum, assessment, children learning English as an additional language, translation and interpreting and family involvement.

Any strategy aimed at countering racism by addressing identified concerns needs a clear framework. The framework will have key elements, or components, each of which address particular areas of responsibility. These components interlock like links in a chain, they are dependent on each another and are designed to address responsibilities and their implications. For example, part of a chain that has links across a whole early years service might be:

1 ensure that resources for play in all settings are appropriate (*leads to*)
2 devise criteria for evaluating the resources (*leads to*)
3 appoint management personnel to monitor the use of resources across the service (*leads to*)
4 ensure that all settings are aware of the criteria for evaluating resources and the process for monitoring them (*leads to*)
5 train staff in settings so they know what to look for when evaluating resources (*leads to*)
6 appoint suitable trainers (*leads to*)
7 include funding for this kind of training in the budget.

These interlinked issues will be supported by others, for instance the need to establish

56 | Action for racial equality in the early years

monitoring mechanisms to ensure that resources for play are checked regularly. Family members, and others involved, will also be encouraged to share the principles and process of what it means to provide their children with appropriate resources for play. The links are endless.

Any framework must incorporate components that will ensure racial equality is put into practice in all aspects of early years services and settings and identify where the responsibility for implementing policies lies. The components should define and describe what needs to be done and who is to do it.

Commitment is the key. Trying to implement racial equality without commitment will not work. Individual people at every level in the service will determine whether it works or not.

A framework of interlinked components

In this handbook, six components of an overall framework have been devised and appear on pages 58–59. Other frameworks with fewer or more components could be adapted from the one here.

The framework is written in some detail, but this does not mean that every part is of equal importance or that every item should be dealt with immediately. It is a framework to work towards and is intended to be helpful rather than daunting. Every Partnership, early years service and early years setting is unique. To be effective, the framework should be adapted for each situation but should keep the basic principles in mind. While the objectives may be idealistic, realism must prevail. It takes time to reach the ideal.

Essential knowledge

To effectively implement a policy framework for racial equality, people working with children or in the early years service, or Partnership members, will need to have some knowledge and understanding of issues listed below. (Many of these issues are dealt with throughout this book and, where appropriate, cross references have been provided for major discussions on a specific issue.)

The law
- The Race Relations Act 1976, and the concepts of direct and indirect discrimination and positive action (see pages 47–50).

Facts about racism
- The facts of racial discrimination and disadvantage in Britain today.[62]

- The history of British racism and the legacy it leaves today (see pages 29–32).
- The effect of racism on both white and black children (see pages 12–15).
- The way that cultural assumptions, stereotypes and adult expectations may limit children's equal access to the full range of learning resources (see pages 9–11).
- The nature of racial harassment (including name-calling) and how it can be addressed (see Chapter 8).

Anti-discriminatory policies
- Anti-racist practice in early years settings (see Chapter 6).
- Effective policymaking, writing programmes, collecting, monitoring and evaluating ethnic data, and consultation with families.
- The role of effective training in the implementation of racial equality.
- The importance of using appropriate terminology (see pages Chapter 3).
- The issues involved in groups working together, respecting a variety of opinions, establishing an atmosphere of trust and empathy, ensuring that the views of all families are heard (see pages 38–40).
- Establishing a no-blame culture which addresses issues of racial equality so that others can understand and accept the need for change without feeling guilty or uncomfortable about speaking (see pages 38–40).

Working with children
- Ways of helping children to unlearn racially prejudiced attitudes and behaviour, and to learn positive attitudes to racial differences (see pages 41–44).[63]
- The importance of helping children to be 'critically aware' of the world around them and how this can best be achieved (see pages 41–44).
- What to look for in assessing children's learning resources on racial equality issues (see pages 41–42).
- The advantages of bilingualism and learning to be bilingual and the current methods of teaching English as an additional language (see pages 22–25).

Working with the community
- The vital role that family members play in the development of children's racial attitudes, with a consideration of how best to involve them, in complementary ways, in working together towards all children having positive racial attitudes (see pages 34–38).

Planning for equality across the early years service | **57**

Sample framework

Framework objective: An Early Years Development and Childcare Plan should provide racial equality in employment and all services for young children and their families.

The linked components needed to satisfy this objective might include the following.

Framework component	*What does the component actually mean?*
1 All Partnership members should be involved in, and committed to, devising, implementing and monitoring policies for racial equality as part of their Early Years Development and Childcare Plan for the service.	Responsibility for ensuring that racial equality is implemented in practice in the early years service and the settings included in the plan lies with the Partnership members. Part of this responsibility is to ensure that the views of black families and the families of Travellers, refugees and asylum seekers are represented on the Partnership and that these families are fully consulted about their wishes for the plan.
2 All those working in the early years service should be responsible to the Partnership for ensuring that the policies are implemented and monitored effectively.	All those staff working in the service, not including those in the early years settings, are responsible for ensuring that the policies of the Partnership are implemented in practice, both in the service itself and in all the settings.
3 The Partnership and the early years service should ensure that all people working with children in early years settings, management, governors, committee members, family members and relevant members of the local community should be: • involved in devising the setting's policies and procedures for racial equality; • committed to their implementation and to monitoring their effectiveness.	The Partnership and those working in the service are responsible for ensuring that every setting develops and implements effective policies and procedures for racial equality, with involvement and in full co-operation with governors, management, committee members and family and community members, and supports the setting in putting this into practice.
4 All aspects of the service and the settings should be free of unlawful racial discrimination and aim to counter other forms of racial discrimination that are not covered by the law.	Understanding and taking account of the Race Relations Act 1976, monitoring and evaluating employment and admission arrangements by collecting ethnic data and considering practices and procedures that might be discriminatory but are not covered by the law.

Framework component	What does the component actually mean?

5 Everyone working in the service and early years settings, and all children and their families involved in the settings, should be treated with equal concern.

Ensuring that everyone is treated with equal value and respect and with equal regard for their feelings and beliefs. With children it means thinking particularly about every child as an individual and ensuring that each child's needs are addressed. It means examining everything that is around the children – the adults and other children, resources, the overt and hidden curriculum – and ensuring that each child has equal access to the full range of learning opportunities. It requires more than simply making sure everyone has appropriate resources, it is about making sure that everyone's specific and general needs are addressed and that a watchful eye is kept on every child to check that they have access to all the learning resources available.

6 Strategies should be developed to support all children and adults in:
- learning positive attitudes and behaviour to those different from themselves;
- countering any negative attitudes and behaviour to differences that they may have already learned.

Recognising that adults and children usually reflect their personal environments in their racial attitudes. Unless their environment is positive towards racial differences it is likely that they will hold the attitudes which are prevalent in our society, that is racially prejudiced attitudes. They will have learned some of their attitudes and behaviour to differences from many sources outside the early years service or the setting.

The adults in the service should be committed to the Partnership policies and the adults in the settings have a particular responsibility to ensure that the children with whom they work are provided with opportunities for learning positive attitudes to racial differences. They are also responsible for ensuring that any negative attitudes are countered in positive, sensitive and constructive ways.

This component requires people working with children to devise ways of enabling children to consider their attitudes and beliefs in the light of balanced and accurate information. It means providing children with the skills to be 'critically aware' of the world around them, to empathise and reflect, so they have a basis on which to make up their own minds about concepts of fairness and justice. This is particularly important in settings unfamiliar with cultural, linguistic, religious and racial diversity.

Planning for equality across the early years service | **59**

Implementing the policy framework

Policies, programmes and curriculum changes take time and thought to consider. The important thing is to start the process. The points listed below under Component headings address the six components of the framework on pages 58–59. There is a lot to think about. The workings of the framework as a whole need to be considered by Partnership members and others involved in organising an early years service. For those of you working in individual settings, it is worth identifying the components that relate most to your working situation. Think about the points which need your most immediate attention – and who might be able to help you with them – within the context of the whole framework.

Component 1

All Partnership members should be involved in and committed to devising, implementing and monitoring policies for racial equality as part of their Early Years Development and Childcare Plan for the service.

- Consider the implications for the Partnership, early years service and settings of the DfEE requirements for an equal opportunity strategy.
- Consider whether membership of the Partnership reflects the views of families from black and minority ethnic communities. If not, take action to address this.
- Devise a policy for racial equality for the Early Years Development and Childcare Plan.
- Devise a policy on racial harassment as part of the plan's policy, with implementation procedures and monitoring mechanisms.
- Devise a programme for implementing the plan's policy – to cover who does what and over what timescales, to define outcomes and monitor mechanisms, resources available and ongoing consultation methods.
- Ensure that at least one Partnership member is familiar with race-related legislation and takes responsibility for racial equality issues.
- Try to ensure that every Partnership member takes responsibility for the policy.
- Establish a database. Collect ethnic data on existing early years settings for children and those working with them, potential future users in the local community, the Partnership members, the early years service staff and all arrangements for employment (recruitment, promotion and access to benefits) and admissions to early years settings.
- Monitor and evaluate this data regularly and identify any discrepancies and possible racial discrimination.
- Devise procedures for rectifying any racial discrimination found.

- Consider taking any relevant positive action under the Race Relations Act and, if necessary, set targets to be achieved by that action.
- Review the policy, implementation and monitoring methods regularly.
- Consider and plan for any training needs in order to implement the strategy, including in recruitment and admissions to settings.
- Encourage governors, management, committee members of early years settings to reflect the ethnic composition of the local community and to support the setting's policy on racial equality.
- Try to build up an ethos of constructive communication and trust between Partnership members within a no-blame culture.
- Budget for and commit resources to implement the policy.

Component 2

All those working in the early years service should be responsible to the Partnership for ensuring that the policies are implemented and monitored effectively.

- All staff in the early years service need to consider the implications for the service of the DfEE requirements for the equal opportunity strategy.
- Ensure that all staff know about, understand and are committed to the policy and implementation programme for racial equality, devised by the Partnership.
- Ensure that all appointments in the service and settings include a person specification about the need for knowledge, commitment and understanding of the policy.
- Ensure that at least one member of staff is familiar with race-related legislation and has responsibility for racial equality issues.
- Ensure that the ethnic database is kept up to date, monitored regularly and any discrepancies identified, and that reports are made to the Partnership on a regular basis.
- Remove any discrimination and identify any possible 'targets' to be achieved by implementing the policy.
- In co-operation with the Partnership, undertake regular reviews of the policy, implementation and monitoring mechanisms and their implications for the service.
- Regularly identify and use sources of support, information, advice and training, and make them available to all staff in the service and all those working in the early years settings.
- Use registration and inspection procedures to raise issues of racial equality with people working in early years settings in a supportive way, helping them to put racial equality into practice.

60 | Action for racial equality in the early years

- Identify any training needs in order to implement the strategy – in the service as a whole and in early years settings.
- Inform the Partnership of training needs and work with them to budget for such training.
- Ensure that space at meetings is given for issues of concern about racial equality to be raised.
- Try to build up an ethos where issues of racial equality and racism can be discussed openly and honestly within a no-blame culture.

Component 3

The Partnership and the early years service should ensure that all people working with children in early years settings, management, governors, committee members, family members, children and relevant members of the local community should be:

- *involved in devising the setting's policies and procedures for racial equality;*
- *committed to their implementation and to monitoring their effectiveness.*

In full and active consultation with all the people working with children, management, governors, committee members, family members, children and relevant members of the local community, devise the following.

- A policy for racial equality, to cover all aspects of the organisation and practice of the setting, including employment, involvement of volunteers, admissions, assessment, translation and interpreting, the curriculum and a strategy for countering the learning of racist attitudes.
- A programme for implementing the policy – including timescale, allocation of responsibilities and details of the practice – in employment and services for young children and their families.
- A policy to address racial harassment and other incidents, including implementation and monitoring procedures and family involvement.
- An ongoing monitoring and analysis mechanism to ensure the policy is being implemented in practice at all levels. This will involve the collection of ethnic data.
- Procedures for rectifying any discrimination found as a result of the analysis.
- A mechanism for raising issues of concern at meetings with those working with children, family members and members of the relevant local communities.
- A budgeting mechanism for implementing the policy to ensure that, so far as possible, no financial constraints limit its implementation.
- Programme meetings of management, governors, committee members, those working with children and families to review, address and consider the

policy and programme of implementation on a regular basis.
- A plan for any training necessary in order to implement the policy (including all budget considerations).
- Ensure that everyone working with children is able to describe, justify and communicate the setting's approach to racial equality issues with parents and family members, children, governors, management, committee members and members of the local community.
- A policy ensuring that children's records are as full as possible, including relevant information on ethnicity, religion (if any), language(s) spoken and language(s) spoken at home, details of the child's developing language capabilities and the child's full name, with the personal and family names identified.
- Methods of ensuring that new parents and family members are introduced to the policy with sensitivity and given opportunities for sufficient time and discussion to understand its implications for them.

Component 4

All aspects of the service and the settings should be free of unlawful racial discrimination and aim to counter other forms of racial discrimination that are not covered by the law.

- Ensure that everyone understands the basis and implications of the Race Relations Act 1976 and what constitutes direct and indirect discrimination.
- Ensure that an experienced person is responsible for racial equality issues, for understanding what constitutes unlawful racial discrimination in detail and what forms of discrimination are not unlawful but are unacceptable, for example racist name-calling between children.
- Ensure that everyone understands the less obvious forms of unlawful racial discrimination, including incidents of less favourable treatment in the curriculum of early years settings, for example as a result of racial stereotyping or provision of limited access to the full range of learning resources. Less favourable treatment can only usually be identified by careful observation and recording.
- Collect data on the ethnic origins of:
  - the children and all those working in the service or the settings;
  - people who apply for and are offered jobs;
  - people who gain employment, promotion and access to in-service support and training;
  - people who apply to attend the setting and who are offered places;
  - all forms of assessment and tests;
  - any exclusions.

Planning for equality across the early years service | **61**

- Analyse this data to identify any discrepancies. Compare the success rates of the various ethnic groups in employment, access to benefits and admissions. If any group is failing disproportionately to be offered a job, a place in a setting or something else, examine the possible reasons for this.
- Remove any discrimination found. Continue to monitor the data to ensure that no discrimination remains.
- Compare the ethnic composition of the workers in the service and the settings, and the children in the setting, with the ethnic composition of the local relevant community. If one does not reflect the other at all levels, check what might be the reasons. For example, are people from some black groups not applying for places in the early years setting and jobs in the service? If not, try to find out why and, if appropriate, seek to change it. Consider using the 'positive action' sections of the Race Relations Act or setting targets to address any discrepancies, if appropriate.
- Examine the admission arrangements and criteria for places in the settings, and the job descriptions and person specifications for jobs to see if any criteria, any work experience, qualifications or requirements are potentially discriminatory (directly or indirectly). For example, are tests given to applicants that might be culturally biased? Is any qualification or experience required for jobs that people from a particular ethnic group would be less likely to have than others? Are any such requirements justified? Are the ways that any waiting lists operate unfair to certain black or other minority ethnic groups?
- Ensure that all vacancies for jobs and for early years settings are widely advertised.
- Examine how the admission criteria are put into practice. Is the way it is done open to everyone?
- Consider whether there is any discrimination in other aspects of the service, for example in the available resources, curriculum (hidden or overt) or training.
- Consider whether there might be forms of discrimination that are not unlawful, for example, name-calling and the omission of appropriate diets and learning resources reflecting the cultures of many of the children in the settings.
- Ensure that all of those involved in the recruitment of workers are trained in equality principles. Those involved in the process – in devising the application form, placing the advertisement, drawing up the job description and person specification, and in shortlisting, interviewing, appointing and giving feedback to applicants – need to be trained about issues of equality.[64]

Component 5

Everyone working in the service and early years settings, and all children and their families involved in the settings, should be treated with equal concern.

The workplace and early years settings should be safe places, free of harassment, where everyone is valued and treated with equal respect and concern. The principles and objectives of the policy for racial equality are the same, whether the area is largely white or multiracial, although some of the practice may be different.

- Examine resources. All resources including toys, books, posters, dolls, play materials, jigsaws, puzzles, miniature play people, colouring and art materials, paper and games need to be examined to ensure they are free of stereotyping, reflect all members of our society accurately, in all walks of life and do not ignore some completely, do not reinforce exotica and any images tell the same story as the text.
- Translate and interpret information, where appropriate, for families who do not speak or read English. Find out where to get material translated into other languages and how to access an interpreter. Consider making a video for families who may not read, for example, Traveller families.
- Value differences positively. Organise projects to talk about, look at, illustrate, recognise and equally value the range of different skin colours, hair colours, textures and styles, and eye, nose and mouth shapes. Talk about concepts of 'beauty' and try to address both the concept itself (ie, why do we 'appear' to value some physical attributes more than others and is this acceptable?) and the ethnocentric concepts of what is considered to be beautiful (ie, the way that blonde-haired, blue-eyed, pale skin are often seen as the most desirable in white British society). Make sure a range of crayons, paints and thinners are available.
- Encourage children to view differences as just that. Avoid reinforcing the message that people who are 'different' are 'exotic', rather than being a part of our world.
- Acknowledge the reality of multicultural, multifaith, multilingual and multiracial Britain on a regular basis and not just when festivals are being 'celebrated'.
- Have high expectations of every child, free of stereotypes. Analyse practice, observe children and record what they do and how they relate to adults to ensure that each is expected to succeed intellectually, socially, physically and emotionally.

- Actively ensure that all children's self-esteem is promoted by positively valuing them personally, their cultural and racial background, their skin colour and their families. Make it clear that all this is treasured in the setting.
- Allow and encourage all children to play all roles. Ensure that particular roles are not always perceived as only being able to be performed by a child of a particular colour. For example, a black child could play Cinderella but, perhaps, not Goldilocks (though neither could a brown-haired white child).
- Observe and monitor children's interactions. Watch carefully what children do and say to each other to ensure that racially prejudiced remarks or behaviour are identified and addressed. Observe who is included and who is excluded and deal with anything that is excluding anyone on racial grounds. If children of the same racial group appear to stay together, try to find out why. It may be because of a common cultural understanding and sense of belonging, but it may be because they do not feel welcomed and valued by children of other racial groups. Children of any racial group may be subjected to prejudice, not only black children by white children. Involve parents in addressing such circumstances.
- Deal with all incidents of racial harassment, however 'insignificant' they might seem. A racist incident is one where a person is subjected to negative treatment because of the racial group to which they belong. It may range from 'unintentionally' saying something negative about someone, to making offensive racist remarks or even racist physical abuse or violence.
- Devise a policy against harassment (see Chapter 8).
- Be constantly aware of how easy it is to jump to conclusions, to make assumptions about a person or people. For example, regarding how people spend their leisure time, what time their children go to bed or what clothes they dress their children in to come to the setting.
- Think about what terminology is used in the early years setting. Check that it is not reinforcing racism and that it is not offensive to anyone. Create an atmosphere where people can say what they find offensive and why, and where other people will listen to what is said with respect and not resentment or a defensive reaction. Listen carefully to what children, those working with children and family members say and, where appropriate, deal with any offensive terminology in a forward-looking and non-threatening way.
- Consider the variety of child-rearing practices. Find out as much as possible about the range of child-rearing practices used by families in the early years setting and elsewhere. In thinking about them and discussing them with colleagues, evaluate their role in the variety of cultural groups and assess what others can learn from this variety. Use the information to begin to break down racial hierarchies of what are often believed to be the 'best' ways to bring up children.
- Consider the overt (explicit) and the covert (hidden) curriculum. Examine whether there are any differences between what is overt and what might be more subtle influences in the curriculum. The resources, the adult–child and adult–adult relationships, and what is not said or not done may give covert messages to children about who is important and valued in the setting and elsewhere.
- Consider the ethnic composition of the children and the people working with them. Does it reflect the ethnic composition of the local community? If there are discrepancies, is this due to factors that the early years setting needs to address? For example, are the vacancies for jobs and places in the setting widely advertised? Are the selection and admission criteria fair? Is it necessary to take some positive action to rectify any discrepancies? (See section on positive action, page 49.)
- Observe, monitor and evaluate which children are doing what. Consider whether every child is, in practice, having an opportunity to learn from and experience all the aspects of the curriculum to be able to develop the full range of learning skills. Observe and record what every child does on a regular basis. Evaluate the access that each child has to the curriculum.
- Observe and evaluate adult–child and adult–adult relationships. Not every child can relate happily to every member of staff, not every member of staff can relate happily to every child, and not all of the people working with children will relate happily to each other. But every adult and every child must be treated equally. This means observing, with open minds, the way everyone relates to each other, to ensure that this is being put into practice. Recognising and accepting that no one is perfect and that everyone finds some aspects of life, including life in the early years setting, difficult is important. This is not easy to do and can only be put into practice when there is a no-blame culture (see pages 38–40).
- Think about multiculturalism. Are all the resources and curriculum plans recognising, taking account of and addressing the fact that cultures in Britain are ranked in a racial hierarchy and are not equally valued by everyone?

Planning for equality across the early years service | **63**

- Think about the ethos of the setting. A short visit can result in a superficial impression which may or may not be correct. A hunch about whether a setting has a 'good feeling' may not be accurate. More thought should be put into an evaluation. What would someone coming in really think about what the setting was doing? What are the 'messages' given to a visitor? By analysing things, what are the components that comprise and define the ethos? Does this closer analysis confirm or deny the initial impression? What needs to be done to ensure that both the ethos and the analysis give positive messages about countering racism?

Component 6

Strategies should be developed to support all children and adults in:

- *learning positive attitudes and behaviour to those different from themselves;*
- *countering any negative attitudes and behaviour to differences that they may have already learned.*

In order to have early years services and settings that are based upon principles of racial equality and justice, discrimination must be removed and every child must be treated with equal concern. There is also a need to address the way racism is passed on from generation to generation in our society. Unless some action is taken to break this cycle, it is likely to continue.

Early years settings provide the opportunity to support and encourage children to value people different from themselves as well as those similar to themselves. It is also an opportunity to help children unlearn any racially prejudiced attitudes and behaviour that they may have already learnt.

While staff may be working very hard to counter racism, the influences of racism outside a setting still have an effect on what goes on inside. Children reflect their environments and bring their racial attitudes to the setting, so there is a need to intervene in the learning and re-learning process of racist attitudes and to give children the opportunity to consider what they are learning in the light of their experiences. This should provide them with skills to seek out information before arriving at a conclusion – the basis for future academic learning at school – and give them the opportunity to make up their own minds about what they think is fair and just.

It is important to be particularly sensitive about the way this work is undertaken as it is all too easy for people to misinterpret the reasons for it, or to undermine implementation of a policy. Be clear about why it is necessary and involve families, children, governors, management and committee members at all stages as partners in the policy for racial equality.

Parents and families are particularly important here. Without their support and commitment the chance of success is hugely reduced.

- Know about and understand, as far as possible, the origins of racism. This will help to explain why work in largely white areas is as important as elsewhere. It will also explain how racism first took a hold, who benefited from it, how myths and stereotypes were built up and the mechanisms used to pass on the attitudes and beliefs that have sustained it over the years.
- Think about how families can be involved in working for racial equality. Families are the most critical influences on children's thinking and lives. In agreeing to, and supporting, the policy for equality they will already have experienced some discussion and received information on the issues. Only by engaging them in the programme to counter the learning of racist attitudes will it have a real chance of success.
- Talk with children about what they think and believe. Talk with them about their attitudes to differences. If you don't know what they think, you won't be able to identify any need to provide them with other information or to raise issues with them or their parents. Be informed and confident as to how a situation or conversation might emerge so that effective and supportive discussion can take place. Take particular care to ensure that any discussion does not blame anyone but that it addresses the issue, not the child personally. (See the section on a no-blame policy, pages 38–40.)
- Plan a programme to introduce children to the wider world in which we live. Provide accurate information about the world. Think about and identify the commonly held stereotypical images of what the world is like.
- Provide opportunities for children to hear and consider a variety of viewpoints. In order to learn how to consider conflicting pieces of information objectively, children need the experience of understanding how to evaluate them. What questions do they need to ask, what further information should they seek and what criteria are they using to make their judgements? The ability to evaluate can be encouraged through exercises that are completely unrelated to anti-discrimination, for instance by asking children to suggest venues for a forthcoming outing, compiling a list from their suggestions, then asking them for their views on the good and bad points of each venue (their *reasons* for wanting or not wanting to visit each place). The children then vote for their favourite venue, and of course go on the trip itself. This kind of process can be referred to at any time.

64 | Action for racial equality in the early years

- Develop strategies to raise issues of concern, to empower children to question conflict and help them address it positively. The experience of everyday practice will highlight issues that need to be addressed strategically. For example, if all children in the setting are white, there will be lots of work to be done to raise awareness, empathy and factual knowledge of people from other racial groups. This might be started by a project on food or dress or languages – things that everyone can join in with. Such a project would simply be focusing on the different ways that people who all live and work in Britain go about their daily lives. Monitoring of the racial incidents record may reveal issues that need to be considered. It may also be important to encourage all children to participate equally in discussions and storytelling. Circle time can be the basis for this, where each child is responsible for the wellbeing of the others.
- Provide children with the skills to be critically aware, to empathise and reflect, so that they have a basis on which to make up their own minds about concepts of fairness and justice. Most of the points raised above contribute to the development of these skills. Respect for all children and encouraging them to think, to listen, to change their minds without feeling foolish and to learn in an atmosphere of mutual support and trust will foster the conditions where these skills can be best learned.

Making it all work

There are no magic ways of countering racism and many people may feel disheartened by trying to do it and not getting very far.

Only a strategic approach with a commitment to implementing racial equality throughout the early years service – from central government to every early years setting – has any chance of effecting real change. That is the challenge and the task for the next millennium.

Useful addresses and contacts

Access to Information on Multicultural Education Resources (AIMER)

Reading and Language
  Information Centre
University of Reading
Bulmershe Court
Earley
Reading RG6 1HY
tel 0118 931 8820

AIMER is a database which provides access to information on multicultural education resources.

Anti-Racist Teacher Education Network (ARTEN)

c/o Samidha Garg
28 Shendish Edge
London Road
Apsley
Hemel Hempstead
HP3 9SZ

This is a national network committed to improving the quality of teacher education for the benefit of staff, students and children.

Black Childcare Network

c/o Hearsay
17 Brownhill Road
Catford
London SE6 2EG

The Black Childcare Network works in a voluntary capacity to raise and share issues of concern to black people working with and caring for young children.

Commission for Racial Equality (CRE)

Elliot House
10/12 Allington Street
London SW1E 5EH
tel 0171 828 7022

The Commission works towards the elimination of discrimination and the promotion of equality of opportunity. It offers advice, information and, where appropriate, support to individuals and groups.

Community Insight

The Pembroke Centre
Swindon SN2 2PQ
tel 01793 512612

Community Insight is a specialist bookseller in early childhood education and playwork.

Early Years Trainers Anti Racist Network (EYTARN)

PO Box 28
Wallasey L45 9NP
tel 0151 639 6136

This is a national network of people working to encourage anti-racist practices in the education and care of young children. It organises campaigns for equality and justice, holds conferences, publishes relevant information and materials, acts as a consultant on training and making videos, offers advice and support, responds to proposed and existing legislation and publishes a newsletter. Together with nine other European countries, it has produced guidelines for trainers and teachers on an anti-bias approach in the early years.

Equality Learning Centre

356 Holloway Road
London N7 6PA
tel 0171 700 8127

The Equality Learning Centre is a resource and development centre offering information and training on children's rights and equality in the early years. It is open to anyone interested in practical ways to work towards equality and children's participation. The information service answers queries on equality issues and empowerment in early years provision. There is a small reference library and resource centre with a unique collection of books, videos, periodicals, resources packs and toys.

Language or multi-ethnic curriculum support services

Although not established specifically for work in the early years, many local education authorities are responsible for language support services for children who are learning English as an additional language and curriculum support services for all children about our multiracial, multifaith, multicultural, multilingual society. These are staffed by teachers, bilingual support staff and others, usually under specific funding, working both in their centres and in schools. While their brief is to concentrate specifically on working with minority ethnic children, they have tried to widen out their concerns to work with all children. Many have worked in early years provision and most have been influential in raising issues about racism wherever they were able to do so. They have, wherever possible, given limited funding, and organised and run courses about racism for early years staff.

The role of bilingual classroom assistants working in nurseries

66 | Action for racial equality in the early years

has been crucial, both in providing a multiracial workforce and providing access to the curriculum for children learning English as an additional language. This has been a lifeline for many children. Critically and significantly, most of these centres have well-stocked resources, often providing the only effective access to resources for teachers and others in their areas. These centres have often been the focus of anti-racist work in local authorities as well as being some of the very few places where black and bilingual staff have been employed in significant numbers.

Letterbox Library
Unit 2D
Leroy House
436 Essex Road
London N1 3QP
tel 0171 226 1633

Letterbox Library is a non-profit-driven co-operative which supplies quality multicultural, non-sexist and special interest titles that have been pre-selected by an independent panel of teachers, librarians and parents. The selection is unique, with many titles unavailable elsewhere. It is often used by training colleges, advisers and inspectors.

Local Authorities Race Relations Information Exchange (LARRIE)
Layden House
76/86 Turnmill Street
London EC1M 5QU
tel 0171 296 6779

This national charity provides information to help local authorities initiate, develop and monitor their strategies for racial equality. It offers access to a database containing all aspects of local authority service provision and employment practices.

Multicultural resources centres
Many LEAs have multicultural resource centres, perhaps as part of their professional or teachers' development centres. See the phone book for LEA address.

National Association for Language Development in the Curriculum (NALDIC)
South Hertforshire LCSC
Holywell School Site
Tolpits Lane
Watford WD1 8NT
tel 01923 231855

NALDIC is a professional organisation concerned with the achievement of bilingual pupils. It disseminates information and represents the views of teachers and other professions on educational issues that affect the teaching and learning of bilingual pupils

Racial Equality Councils
Most areas have a local council for racial equality which provides local information on organisations and resources. See the phone book for address.

REU (formely the Race Equality Unit)
Unit 27/28, Angel Gate
City Road
London EC1V 2PT
tel 0171 278 2331

This is an organisation promoting black people's right to services which are accessible, appropriate, accountable and adequate. In its work with children it also addresses issues of racial equality in early years services. It undertakes training, consultancy, research and development, project work, national conferences and workshops, publications, resource

facilities and networking with black individuals and organisations.

Reading and Language Information Centre
The University of Read ng
Bulmershe Court
Earley
Reading RG6 1HY
0118 931 8820

A unit within the University of Reading that provides advice through courses, conferences and publications on all aspects cf language and literacy learning.

Working Group Against Racism in Children's Resources (WGARCR)
460 Wandsworth Road
London SW8 3LX
0171 627 4594

This is a nationwide network of people working to remove racist images and stereotypes from children's books, toys and other learning resources because of their damaging effects on all children. It aims to identify resources that reinforce racism and adopt appropriate strategies for their removal. It encourages the production and use of non-racist resources. It campaigns on specific issues and responds to inquiries from teachers, carers, parents, librarians and others. It organises regular conferences on a range of issues, including children's racial identity and the Children Act. It publishes selection criteria for toys and books and trains and advises publishers, suppliers and others on their use. It marked the European Year Against Racism and Xenophobia by conducting a survey to measure the success of the struggle against racism in children's resources. As part of its work it aims to set up regional support groups.

Notes

1 Department for Education and Employment (1998) *Early Years Development and Childcare Partnership: planning guidance 1999–2000*, DfEE, London.

2 Kutner, B. (1958) 'Patterns of mental functioning associated with prejudice in children', *Psychological monographs*, vol. 72.

3 Bloom, L. (1971) *The social psychology of race relations*, George Allen & Unwin, London.

4 Alibhai, Y. (1987) 'The child racists', *New society*, 4 December.

5 Williams, P. (1997) 'The genealogy of race: towards a theory of grace', *The 1997 Reith Lectures*, BBC Radio 4, London.

6 Ammons, R. (1950) 'Reactions in a projective doll-play interview of white males two to six years of age to differences in skin colour and facial features, *Journal of genetic psychology*, vol. 76;

   Clark, K. (1955) *Prejudice and your child*, Beacon Press, Boston: MA;

   Goodman, M. (1952) *Race awareness in young children: a cultural anthropologist's study of how racial attitudes begin among four year olds*, Collier Books, New York;

   Horowitz, E. (1936) 'Development of attitudes towards Negroes', *Archives of psychology*, no. 194;

   Milner, D. (1983) *Children and race: 10 years on*, Ward Lock, London;

   Morland, J. (1962) 'Racial acceptance and preference of nursery school children in a Southern city', *Merrill-Palmer quarterly*, vol. 8;

   Pushkin, I. (1967) 'A study of ethnic choice in the play of young children', unpublished PhD thesis, London;

   Radke, M., Sutherland, J. & Rosenberg, P. (1950) 'Racial attitudes of children, *Sociometry*, vol. 13;

   Stevenson, H. & Stewart, E. (1958) 'A developmental study of racial awareness in young children', *Child development*, vol. 29;

   Vaughan, G. (ed.) (1972) *Racial issues in New Zealand*, Akarana Press, Auckland.

7 Gay, G. (1985) 'Implications of selected models of ethnic identity development for educators', *Journal of Negro education*, vol. 54, no. 1;

8 Maxime, J. (1991) *Towards a transcultural approach to working with under-sevens*, conference report for the Early Years Trainers Anti Racist Network and the National Children's Bureau, EYTARN, Wallasey.

9 Akhtar, S. & Stronach, I. (1986) '"They call me blacky": a story of everyday racism in primary schools', *Times educational supplement*, 9 September.

10 Jay, E. (1992) *Keep them in Birmingham: challenging racism in southwest England*, Commission for Racial Equality, London.

11 Derbyshire, H. (1994) *Not in Norfolk: tackling the invisibility of racism*, Norwich and Norfolk Racial Equality Council, Norwich.

12 British Broadcasting Corporation (1996) 'Rural racism', *Farming today*, BBC Radio, Midlands and East, 25 May.

13 Jones, S. (1993) *The language of the genes: biology, history and the evolutionary future*, HarperCollins, London.

14 Brain, J. & Martin, M. (1983) *Child care and health for nursery nurses*, Hulton Educational, London.

15 Pollack, M. (1972) *Today's three year olds in London*, Heinemann, London.

16 Sandler, G. (1972) unpublished letter to the Community Relations Commission.

17 Coard, B. (1971) *How the West Indian child is made educationally subnormal in the British school system*, New Beacon Books, London.

18 Van der Eyken, W. (1984) *Day nurseries in action*, Department of Child Health Research Unit, University of Bristol, Bristol.

19 Working Group Against Racism in Children's Resources (1991) *Guidelines for the evaluation and selection of child development books*, WGARCR, London.

20 Doughty, S. (1988) 'Racist check on toddlers', *Daily Mail*, 6 October, page 1.

21 Hardyment, C. (1996) 'Toytown gone mad', *The Daily Telegraph*, 13 April, page 1 of Weekend section.

22 Edwards, V. (1996) *The other languages: a guide to multilingual classrooms*, Reading and Language

Information Centre, Reading.

23 Dalby, D. (1997) 'Global study finds the world speaking in 10,000 tongues', *The Guardian*, 22 July.

24 Baker, C. (1997) *Foundations of bilingual education and bilingualism*, Multilingual Matters, Clevedon.

25 Department of Education and Science (1967) *Children and their primary schools: a report of the Central Advisory Council for Education* ('The Plowden Report'), HMSO, London.

26 Her Majesty's Stationery Office (1985) *Education for all: report of the Committee of Inquiry into the education of children from ethnic minority groups* ('The Swann Report'), HMSO, London.

27 Her Majesty's Stationery Office (1989) *The Children Act – Guidance and regulations: Volume 2, Family support, day care and educational provision for young children*, HMSO, London.

28 Office for Standards in Education (1998) *Nursery education inspection: guidance on equality of access and opportunity*, Ofsted, London.

29 School Curriculum and Assessment Authority (1996) *Nursery education: desirable outcomes for children's learning – on entering compulsory education*, SCAA, London.

30 Early Childhood Education Forum (1998) *Quality and diversity in early learning*, ECEF, National Children's Bureau, London.

31 Japanese mother living in the USA (1998), *The Guardian*, 18 July.

32 For more information see Zealey, C. (1995) 'The importance of names', in *Coordinate Collection*, National Early Years Network, London.

33 Gutsmore, C. (1995), speaking at a seminar organised jointly by the Black Childcare Network, the Early Childhood Unit of the National Children's Bureau and the Early Years Trainers Anti Racist Network.

34 For further discussion, see Lane, J. (1998) 'Ethnic monitoring: why, how and about what', in Early Years Trainers Anti Racist Network, *Planning for excellence: implementing the DfEE guidance requirement for the equal opportunity strategy in Early Years Development Plans*, EYTARN, Wallasey.

34 Meltzer, H. (1994) *Daycare services for children: a survey carried out on behalf of the Department of Health in 1990*, Office of Population Censuses and Surveys, Social Survey Division, HMSO, London.

35 Kenway, P. (1994) *Working with parents*, Save the Children in association with Reading and Language Information Centre;

Early Years Trainers Anti Racist Network (1995) *Partnership with parents: an anti-discriminatory approach*, EYTARN, Wallasey;

National Early Years Network (1995) *Playing fair: a parents' guide to tackling discrimination*, NEYN, London;

Ball, M. (1997) *Consulting with parents: guidelines for good practice*, NEYN, London.

36 Department for Education and Employment (1998) *Early Years Development and Childcare Partnership: planning guidance 1999–2000*, DfEE, London.

37 For further discussion see Early Years Trainers Anti Racist Network (1995) *Best of both worlds: celebrating mixed parentage*, EYTARN, Wallasey; and Chambers, C., Funge, S., Harris, G. & Williams, C. (1996) *Celebrating identity: a resource manual*, Trentham Books, Stoke-on-Trent.

38 Office for Standards in Education (1996) *The education of travelling children*, Ofsted, London.

39 Two examples of books that settings might offer to parents are: Pre-school Playgroups Association (1991) *Equal chances: eliminating discrimination and ensuring equality in playgroups*, PPA, London; and Brown, B. (1995) *All our children: a guide for those who care*, BBC Publications, London (available from EYTARN).

40 For helpful support, see Elfer, P. (1995) *With equal concern*, National Children's Bureau, London.

41 For further discussion about working in white areas see Early Years Trainers Anti Racist Network (1993), *Racism: the white agenda*, EYTARN, Wallasey.

42 Local Government Management Board (1998) *Independent workforce survey 1998*, prepared for the Early Years National Training Organisation, the National Private Day Nurseries Association and the Department for Education and Employment, LGMB, London.

43 Dixon, B. (1992) *Playing them false: a study of children's toys, games and puzzles*, Trentham Books, Stoke-on-Trent;

Working Group Against Racism in Children's Resources (1995) *Guidelines for the evaluation and selection of toys and other resources*, WGARCR, London. Other resources are available from Letterbox Library and Community Insight.

44 For more about persona dolls, see Derman Sparks, L. and the ABC Task Force (1989) *Anti-bias curriculum: tools for empowering young children*, National Association for the Education of Young Children, Washington: DC (available from the National Early Years Network); and Creaser, B. & Dau, E. (1996) *The anti-bias approach in early childhood*, Harper Educational, Australia, pages 162–73.

45 Jones, S. (1991) *The 1991 Reith Lectures*, BBC Radio 4.

46 For further information about religious groups and the law, see Commission for Racial Equality (1996) *From cradle to school: a practical guide to racial equality in early childhood education and care*, CRE, London.

47 Department for Education and Employment (1998) *Early Years Development and Childcare Partnership: planning guidance 1999–2000*, DfEE, London.

48 Early Years Trainers Anti Racist Network (1998) *Planning for excellence: implementing the DfEE Guidance requirement for the equal opportunity strategy in Early Years Development Plans*, EYTARN, Wallasey.

49 Qualifications and Curriculum Authority (1998) *Draft framework for qualifications and training in the early years education, childcare and playwork sector*, QCA, London.

50 Office for Standards in Education (1998) *Nursery education inspection: guidance on equality of access and opportunity*, Ofsted, London.

51 Department for Education and Employment (1998) *Early Years Development and Childcare Partnership: planning guidance 1999–2000*, DfEE, London.

52 For detailed information about the Race Relations Act and the Children Act, see Lane, J. (1990) 'Sticks and carrots: using the Race Relations Act to remove bad practice and the Children Act to promote good practice', *Local government policy making,* vol. 1, no. 3. For detailed information about the Children Act, see Lane, J. (1992) 'The 1989 Children Act: a framework for racial equality in children's daycare/education', *Early years,* vol. 12, no. 2.

53 Commission for Racial Equality (1996) *From cradle to school: a practical guide to racial equality in early childhood education and care*, CRE, London.

54 For further information, see Lane, J. (1998) 'Ethnic monitoring: why, how and about what?', in Early Years Trainers Anti Racist Network, *Planning for excellence: implementing the DfEE Guidance requirement for the equal opportunity strategy in Early Years Development Plans*, EYTARN, Wallasey.

55 For further discussion, see Commission for Racial Equality (1991) *Positive action and equal opportunity in employment*, CRE, London.

56 For further discussion see Commission for Racial Equality (1993) *Job advertisements and the Race Relations Act: a guide to Section 5*, CRE, London.

57 This wording is the same as that used in the Home Office criteria for funding under Section 11 of the Local Government Act 1966.

58 For issues about the registration of these groups under the Children Act 1989, see Commission for Racial Equality (1996) *From cradle to school: a practical guide to racial equality in early childhood education and care*, CRE, London.

59 See Early Years Trainers Anti Racist Network (1996) *On the spot: dealing with racism*, EYTARN, Wallasey.

60 Walker, Alice (1989) *The temple of my familiar*, Harcourt Brace Jovanovich, New York.

61 Department for Education and Employment (1997) *Early Years Development Partnerships and Plans: guidance 1998–99*, DfEE, London; Department for Education and Employment (1998) *Early Years Development and Childcare Partnership: planning guidance 1999–2000*, DfEE, London.

62 A useful source of information is Modood, T., Berthoud, R. *et al* (1998) *Ethnic minorities in Britain: diversity and disadvantage. The fourth national survey of ethnic minorities*, Policy Studies Institute, London. For specific details, see the following Commission for Racial Equality Fact sheets: 'Criminal justice in England and Wales'; 'Education and training in Britain'; 'Employment and unemployment'; 'Ethnic minorities in Britain'; 'Ethnic minority women'; 'Housing'; 'Racial attacks'; 'Refugees and asylum seekers'; 'Policing'; 'Young people in Britain', available from CRE Distribution Services, Eliot House, 10–12 Allington Street, London SW1E 5EH.

63 See also Brown, B. (1998) *Unlearning discrimination in the early years*, Trentham Books, Stoke-on-Trent (available from EYTARN).

64 Darling, B. & Hedge, A. (1992) *Fair interviewing*, Trentham Books, Stoke-on-Trent.